A HISTORY OF
WESTERN SCULPTURE

CONSULTANT EDITOR
JOHN POPE-HENNESSY

Sculpture
19th & 20th
Centuries

Fred Licht

MICHAEL JOSEPH · LONDON

© GEORGE RAINBIRD LTD 1967

This book was designed and produced by
George Rainbird Ltd
2 Hyde Park Place, London, W.2

House editor: Jocelyn Selson
Designers: Ronald Clark and George Sharp

Printed by Jarrold & Sons Ltd, Norwich

TO MY PARENTS, MY WIFE
AND FOR MATTHEW,
DANIEL AND SABINA

ILLUSTRATION CREDITS

The publishers acknowledge with gratitude the helpfulness and generosity of museums, private collectors and photographers in all parts of Europe and America in supplying the photographs for this volume. Their names are acknowledged in the captions which indicate the location of the sculptures. Listed below are additional sources, copyright-owners (in italics) and photographers.

AMSTERDAM A.N.E.F.O. (photo) 236, 248

ANGERS *J. Evers* (photo) 53, 56

ANTWERP J. de Maeyer (photo) 326

BARCELONA *Editorial R. M.*, Foto Archives Gomis Prats 151

BASLE Jeck (photo) 267, 269; *Robert Spreng* (photo) 127, 129

BELFORT *Syndicat d'Initiative* 101

BRUSSELS *A.C.L.* (photo) 111

CHICAGO Art Institute 242; J. Howard (photo) VI

COMO *Brunner* (photo) 160

CONNECTICUT E. I. Blomstrann (photo) 243, 245, 247; E. de Cusati (photo) 227; Schiff (photo) 343

COPENHAGEN Jonals (photo) 13, 14, 15, 17

DÜSSELDORF *Dr. Frantz Stoedtner* (photo) 34, 35, 154, 155, 210

FIESOLE Barsotti (photo) 95, 96

FLORENCE *Alinari* (photo) [*Mansell*, London] 5, 11, 47, 48, 49, 66, 100, 109, 129

FRANKFURT a. M Gabriele Busch-Hauck (photo) 37

GOTHENBURG Kennroth (photo) 38

HAMBURG F. Hewicker (photo) 207, 208

LIGORNETTO Christian Senn (photo) 112, 113

LILLE *The Mayor*, La Voix du Nord (photo) 348

LONDON Godwin (photo) 106; *Lord Chamberlain* 24 (photo A. F. Kersting); *Lund Humphries* (*publishers*) 'Henry Moore Sculptures and Drawings' 292 (photo Lidbrooke), 293, 295, 'Hepworth Drawings and Carvings' 297, 'Naum Gabo' 243, 245, 246, 247; *Pitkin* (*publishers*) 99 (photo Sydney Newbery); *George Rainbird* I, 235, 252, 262, 264, 271, 286, 335 (photo Peter Cannon Brookes), 21, 22 (photo Margaret Harker), 36, 110, 236 (photo Keystone), 182 (photo Sotheby & Co); *Tate Gallery*, reproduced by courtesy of the Trustees, IV (photo John Webb), 40, 120, 195, 201; *University College* 20 (photo Helmut Gernsheim); Yugoslav Embassy 156

LÜBECK *Wilhelm Castelli* (photo) 209

LYON J. Camponagara (photo) 31

MADRID *MAS* (photo) 152

MILAN *Alberto and Giovanni Buscaglia* (photo) 18; Mercurio (photo) 316, 317, 318, 319, 320; Gian Sinigaglia (photo) 221; *Vitali,* Mario Perotti (photo) 93

NEW YORK Lee Boltin (photo) 130; *Grace Borgenicht Gallery,* 253 (photo Lionel Friedman); Rudolf Burckhardt (photo) 263, 342, 344; *David Gahr* (photo) 349; *Sydney Janis Gallery* 345; *O. E. Nelson* (photo) 237; Isamu Noguchi (photo) 273; Eric Pollitzer (photo) [*George Rainbird,* London], 124, 332; *Port of New York Authority, U.S. Navy* 102; John D. Schiff (photo) 212; Adolf Studly (photo) 274, 287, 330; Soichi Sunami (photo) 117, 140, 149, 165, 166, 181, 184, 193, 198, 199, 202, 204, 222, 226, 238, 239, 240, 244, 254, 257, 260, 281, 284, 285, 288, 289, 299, 302, 303, 310, 324, 329, 334; Charles Uht (photo) 323

OSLO Tergiens Foto Atelier 162

PARIS *A.D.A.G.P.* V, VII, 171, 172, 173, 174, 175, 176, 177, 178, 179, 180, 186, 187, 188, 189, 190, 191, 192, 193, 194, 196, 197, 198, 199, 200, 201, 230, 231, 232, 241, 267, 268, 269, 270, 271, 278, 279, 280, 281, 282, 283, 291, 300, 301, 302, 303, 310, 311, 312, 313; *Archives Photographiques* 25, 30, 50, 51, 52, 54, 55, 58, 60, 61, 71, 74, 77, 87, 88, 89, 90, 92, 115, 119, 121; Pierre Boucher 308; *Pierre Brassai* (photo) Jacket front, 218, 327; *Bulloz* 28, 57, 59, 73, 79, 172, 344, 346; Editions de Minuit 103; *Giraudon* 65, 67, 82, 91, 104, 107, 137, 142; *Maurice Gobin* (photo) 78; *Henri Guilbaud* (photo) 312; Studio Josse Lalance (photo) [*George Rainbird,* London], i, iv, 33, 63, 64, 86, 91, 105, 158, 214, 231, 232; Marouteau & Cie (photo) 304; Rappho (photo) 122; Studio Maywald (photo) 167, 169; *Services de documentation photographique* vii, 70, 75, 80, 85, 144, 179, 180, 188; *S.P.A.D.E.M.* III, IV, 101, 102, 114, 115, 116, 117, 118, 119, 120, 121, 122, 123, 124, 125, 126, 127, 128, 129, 130, 131, 132, 134, 135, 136, 137, 138, 139, 140, 141, 143, 144, 165, 166, 167, 168, 169, 170, 181, 182, 183, 184, 185, 218, 219, 257, 284, 285, 286, 326, 327, 328, 329, 330; Weill (photo) 267, 269

PHILADELPHIA A. J. Wyatt (photo) VII

ROME *American Battle Monuments Commission, U.S. Signal Corps* (photo) 163; *Anderson* (photo) [*Mansell,* London], 1, 121, 159; *Gabinetto Fotografico Nazionale* 44, 148

ST GALLEN F. Maurer (photo) 336, 338

STOCKHOLM *Ragnar von Holten* (photo) 145

VENICE Foto Caccio 2; Fotografia Ferruzzi 6; Fondazione Giorgio Uni Istituto di Storia dell'Arte 3; Fratelli Pozzo 191 (photo Aschieri), 280; Giacomelli (photo) 216, 217, 306, 321, 333

VIENNA *Bild Archiv der Österreichischer Nationalbibliothek* 10

WILLIAMSTOWN, MASS. *Williams College* 347 (photo Fred Licht)

ZÜRICH Eviline Anker (photo) 266; Hans Heider (photo) 276, 277; *Ernst Scheidegger* (photo) 278, 279, 280, 283

ACKNOWLEDGEMENTS

Without the help of the Biblioteca della Biennale in Venice this book could never have been written. It is to the entire staff of this magnificent library and to its director, Signor Umbro Apolonio, that I wish to extend my sincerest thanks.

By allowing me to study her superb collection of twentieth-century sculptures at leisure and by generously communicating to me all manner of important information concerning the sculptors represented in her museum, Mrs Peggy Guggenheim is responsible for all that the reader may find intriguing in this section of the book.

Of very special value was the advice freely offered by the most knowledgeable scholar of nineteenth-century sculpture I have the pleasure of knowing: Mrs Ruth Mirolli. Her reading of the initial sketches for my text and her constant encouragement advanced my work more than I can say. Professore Corrado Maltese opened up the world of nineteenth-century Italian art, thanks to his unsurpassed publications in this field. I also gained considerable insight into the nature of nineteenth-century Italian sculpture by being allowed to visit the Dupré Collection at Fiesole.

And, as always, countless friends assisted me; above all Professor James Holderbaum of Smith College and Professor Robert Rosenblum of Princeton. But nothing would have come of all my work and of all the help which was accorded me if it had not been for the guiding hand of Miss Jocelyn Selson who never tired of solving seemingly insoluble problems connected with the production of this book.

F. L.

NOTE ON THE NUMBERING OF THE ILLUSTRATIONS

In the Introduction – i, ii, iii
The colour plates   – I, II, III
The monochromes – 1, 2, 3

Where there is more than one illustration on a page the captions and pictures
run from left to right and top to bottom.

CONTENTS

'*Si je n'étais pas conquérant je voudrais être sculpteur.*'
NAPOLÉON

'*Que le bronze éternise la boue.*'
VICTOR HUGO

'*Vous louez toujours ce qui vous plaît! Moi jamais.*'
LA BRUNETIÈRE

INTRODUCTION

In most Western religions the act of creation is primarily a sculptural one. Though painting and architecture also have religious origins, they belong to a later stage of sophistication, developing only after a deliberate, if not always conscious, intellectual process. Painting and architecture require a certain degree of abstract thinking. Sculpture is immediately, sensuously perceived, and exists fully in the world of our direct experience since it exists corporeally. To shape with one's hands, to grasp, to hold, these are primordial impulses of man's infancy. The newly born clutches at objects before it can see them.

Totem, idol, sacred tree . . . to worship in awe objects of peculiarly distinct appearance – this is the beginning of sculpture. To perceive behind physical experience a transcendental power, to find in the chaos of daily experience a manifestation of superior forces which control and order life – that is the essence of the urge to create or admire sculpture. Without invoking a hallowed sensation, sculpture is only one more object in an already cluttered universe. On the other hand, without corporeality the transcendental intuition remains abstract and distant.

Being religious in origin, sculpture is also communal, and always tends towards the monumental because only the monumental dimension can satisfy a large community's need for worshipping the concrete appearance of the divine. Sculpture is, therefore, the logical and primary form of expression solely in those epochs or in those cultures in which a firm religious as well as social structure is adhered to by everyone. Since the conjunction of these elements is bound to be rare, the epochs in which sculpture is the predominating art are few in number. The artist must be a fully accredited, acceptable member of the society he serves because sculpture of a monumental scope depends on the dialogue between the community's need and the artist's ability to satisfy that need. Within the Oceanic and African tribes, in Ancient Egypt, Archaic and Classical Greece, conditions were propitious.

During the Hellenistic period sculpture began to play a secondary role, being no longer an integral communal need, but a vehicle for propaganda or a display of virtuosity. The megalomania of the epoch is symptomatic. The Colossus of Rhodes is a bizarre sculpture intended to impress: it does not fulfil an ideal communal purpose as do the Parthenon sculptures or Archaic *kouroi*. It overwhelms the spectator by its enormity rather than by being the embodiment of a communally shared ideal of the divine.

Rome, too, continued to use sculpture for propagandistic purposes of one sort or another. Size rather than true monumentality was the goal, with the correct representation of visible realities its point of departure. And as the transcendental value of worldly appearance is diminished, the artist, as well as the public, loses interest even in the virtuoso rendering of observable reality. If an emperor is merely a usurper who owes his crown to the power of his soldiers, and is likely to lose it again in the next upheaval – if, in other words, he is no longer a believable incarnation of divine will – his physical appearance is of only temporary, ephemeral interest. The dissolution of the classical world has set in. Reality in and for itself, uninformed by enduring significance, becomes irrelevant and therefore not worth portraying.

The Middle Ages, travailed by constant shifts of population and invasions, were inimical to stable social structures. Not till the mature phases of the Romanesque era was there a return to monumental sculpture, though it was rarely, if ever, capable of independent existence, generally needing the support of architecture. Only the late Gothic and early Renaissance periods witnessed the rebirth of independent monumental sculpture. Sculpture again became the leading form of artistic expression – often a rival with painting in introducing important changes in style. With varying success, varying quality and with widening scope for the expression of the individual artist, this situation continued well into the eighteenth century.

Democracy, industrialization, the logic of secularized history in which events are no longer due to the intervention of God's will but to rationally determinable causes – all these characteristics of the decades leading up to the French Revolution gained absolute predominance in the nineteenth century. Though they brought many benefits to mankind, they brought nothing but catastrophic disorientation to sculpture.

In vain do we look for the sculptural equivalents of David's *Oath of the Horatii* or Goya's *Tres de Mayo*. For various reasons which will be indicated, the painter, being able to work quickly and without prior commission, is able to keep pace with the times. A year after David had completed his *Death of Marat*, Marat, yesterday's idol, had become an arch-enemy. David was forced to hide his painting. If he had been a sculptor, he probably would have just arrived at the point of beginning his commemorative work and, considering the radically changed circumstances, the sculpture would never have been completed.

Aberrations begin to appear at this crucial moment which marks the beginning of modern sculpture.* In some cases reality was substituted for a work of art. For instance, a young opera singer called Mlle Maillart was seated on the high altar of Nôtre-Dame to represent the goddess of Reason. Reduced deathmasks of Marat and other heroes of the revolution were sold in great quantities – the first hint of 'sculpture for the masses', in which the intervention of an artist is excluded in favour of the mechanical process of taking a death-mask and multiplying it. All nineteenth-century sculpture is interesting for its symptoms of a universal malaise; comparatively little of it is interesting for sheer quality.

The sculptor, merely a servant under the *ancien régime*, was freed from servitude by the Revolution, but, by the same token, he was thrown upon his own devices. The painter can survive under these circumstances as illustrator, as did David in his cycles concerning the Napoleonic epic, or as decorator. The sculptor cannot survive because his monumental art, necessitating as it does considerable funds, depends on previous commission. He cannot afford to create bronzes or marbles in the hope of getting his money back in some undetermined future. Besides, the sculptor who once served a clear function now becomes a subversive element within a democratic society: the sculptor deals with the exceptional, and it is just the exceptional which is suspect to democracy because democracy flourishes on subservience to a norm.

*   *   *

The three fundamental commissioners on whom the sculptor had traditionally depended ceased to favour sculpture.

---

* Generally, the word 'modern', when applied to painting, designates work done during and after the Fauvist period (1905–8). Many critics, however, either include post-impressionist painting as modern or, going to another extreme, maintain that Cubism is the true beginning of 'modern' art. With sculpture, it is even more difficult to define the exact historical moment which marks the inception of 'modern' statuary. In this book, the word 'modern' is taken to include that period during which all basic traditional concepts of sculpture were challenged and radically undermined. The peculiarly contemporary problems posed by Canova's major works would seem to entitle him to head the roster of 'modern' sculptors, though Canova himself would have most probably rejected such an honour.

The Church. Shaken by the tremendous internal and external conflicts brought on by the Enlightenment and by the Revolution, the Church had to concentrate all its forces on sheer survival. Besides, the existing churches, with their sculptural programmes, were more than sufficient to serve a diminished flock. More important still, the Church became wary of sculpture because of the facile charges of idolatry which were hurled at it from all sides. It is instructive to read about the circumstances in which the most important religious sculptural commission of the nineteenth century was born. When St Bernadette Soubirous was commanded by the Madonna to place a statue in the grotto of Lourdes, a certain Professeur Fabish of Lyon in 1863 went to visit St Bernadette to take notes of her account of the vision. Returning to Lyon he made his first maquette, which he submitted to St Bernadette for correction, modifying his sculpture in accordance with her instructions. The timidity of the procedure, the hesitation in the face of recording a miracle, the peculiarly journalistic procedure of 'getting the facts straight' are highly indicative of Church attitudes towards sculpture. No wonder that the ultimate product lacks all sense of a sacred apparition, and cannot support comparison with even the most humble votive figure of preceding ages.

The State. Whereas a monarchy, being accountable to no one, could freely spend State funds or finance sculptural projects from the privy purse, the parliamentary State had to take into account the displeasure of an enormous public if it misspent public monies. In raising a monument it had to seek to please not the small minority of connoisseurs, but the 'man in the street' who cared little for sculpture, knew less and, if he had preference at all, it was for a repetition of things with which he was already familiar. Given this combination, the State maintained an academic art based on teachable principles which gained respectability by being vaguely connected with the Classic past. That element of art which could be directly translated into words overwhelmed the more purely artistic motivations for which no rational verbal equivalents exist. Academic art was born.

There was also the difficulty of finding heroes or events or principles to which monuments could be erected. Today's political hero may turn out to be tomorrow's traitor. And how does one set a monument to the basic slogan of nineteenth-century political thought: '*Enrichissez-vous!*'? Even the most naïve subject of monumental sculpture, the hero of the battlefield, becomes problematical. The anonymous soldier who is regimented out of all individual initiative loses his heroic aureole and, since wars are no longer fought in the name of the king (God's temporal representative), the

i *Cemetery of monuments*, Paris

very cause for which the soldier falls is put in doubt. One has recourse, therefore, to the subterfuge of the 'Unknown soldier'. But how does one give form and physiognomy to what is unknown? A post-war competition for a monument to the *Unknown political prisoner* (164) ended in a checkmate. A prize was assigned but the project was never executed. A Hungarian who had been an 'unknown political prisoner' happened to see the winning entry and tried to destroy it. The abstraction, though fitting for a theme which is fundamentally abstract, as all unknown quantities must be, irritated him to the pitch of violence because it in no way corresponded to his own torment. Placed between the equally distasteful possibilities either of doing violence to his artistic convictions or to the memory of the victims he is to commemorate, the great sculptor today prefers to leave such traditional and important subjects aside. Only the arid compromise between architecture and sculpture such as was first envisaged by Sant'Elia (160) can come close to commemorating the arid destinies of today's mass-heroes.

One of the odd proofs of the vacillation of governmental sculpture is the cemetery of monuments which exists in almost every European metropolis.

Sculptures which for political and, sometimes, for aesthetic reasons had to be removed from public view are generally not destroyed but placed in enormous repositories (i) . . . one never knows, they might turn out to be art after all.

The private sponsor. It is on this late-comer to the artistic scene, the industrialist, the rich merchant, the banker, that the survival of sculpture in the nineteenth century really depended.* But again two factors, one economic and the other spiritual, intervened. Even the richest millionaire will be unwilling to spend the sums required for large-scale sculptural projects. Nor is it well-mannered or even judicious to make too public a display of one's wealth. The private sponsor is unlikely to commission major works.

If the economic problem is grave, the spiritual problem is disastrous. Rarely is the self-made man educated to the point of being able to communicate *au pair* with the sculptor. Essentially he distrusts the artist who lives outside the realm of profit and success. Also, he is afraid of making mistakes, and sculptural mistakes are infinitely more embarrassing and difficult to dispose of than those made in the acquisition of painting. The banker or industrialist who wants to gain prestige by interesting himself in art usually does so by buying works of the old masters which, though costly, are culturally safe.

Subject-matter again becomes a problem even in the direct dealing between artist and private commissioner. A portrait bust is the most common item,

---

* Private sponsors existed, of course, prior to the nineteenth century, but both their quality and their quantity as well as their relative importance to the artist were radically different. One cannot possibly confound the Medici, the Tornabuoni or the Strozzi with private patrons of the nineteenth century. The former acted in the capacity of an oligarchy anxious to gain prestige not only for themselves but for the greater glory of their city. Only in Holland of the seventeenth century do we find patrons who were more or less analogous to the private sponsor of the nineteenth century. And here again we find a rapid disintegration of the relationship between sculptor and sponsor as well as a marked decline in current artistic taste. After an enthusiastic support of individualistic artists, demanded by violent patriotic rather than aesthetic sentiment, the truly inventive artist was dropped in favour of the prototype of nineteenth-century *pompiers*. The merchant *élite* of Holland was incapable of sustained interest in the powerfully original art of Rembrandt or of the great landscapists. Instead it sought refuge in the conventional, 'approved' style imported from the French court. Still, the patricians of Amsterdam and Haarlem can hardly be confused with the speculators and industrialists of the nineteenth century. The former had an ingrained culture, a respect for learning and a relatively high sense of civic duty which are noticeably absent in the potential art-sponsors of the nineteenth century.

Even the Parisian financier of eighteenth-century Paris, the most direct ancestor of the nineteenth-century collector, was a species distinct from his heirs. He was militantly conscious of his political, historic and cultural position, which the nineteenth-century banker rarely was, and made use of his artist-friends in much the same way as the monarch in Versailles made use of his staff of artists: to consolidate his prestige and his power. The newly maturing *bourgeoisie* was endowed with a vitality, a curiosity and an intelligence which made it rush eagerly into all those cultural fields which had not yet been monopolized by the aristocracy.

but, since the average sitter has little to recommend him except his wealth, the really dedicated master will find little to interest him. Other subjects are even more difficult. What, for instance, can one do with a statuette of a saint? Or a nude? If the saint is really saintly, he destroys the harmony of the sumptuous nineteenth-century living-room. If the nude is really nude, it is inadmissible for nineteenth-century mores.

Born out of this conjuncture of economic and spiritual antagonism there arises a *genre* that is characteristic of the nineteenth century: the so-called art-bronze or statuette.★ Being small, it is easily ranged with lamps, vases and clocks; neutral in subject-matter, it is uncompromising for its owner; impeccable in execution, it is appealing in a decorative way (ii). This latter element is also symptomatic of another trend: the love for precious materials such as gilt bronze, alabaster, onyx and so on. For workmanship and materials alike are factors which can be directly appraised and appreciated even by the most unversed of collectors. They represent an intrinsic worth which makes sense to a collector whose prosperity stems from his knowledge of intrinsic values.

The sculptor who is preferred, the sculptor who determines the market in sculpture, therefore, is generally the one who comes closest to the most avidly collected items: old master bronzes. Probably the great forgers (Dossena, Bastianini, Ruchomowski) made more money on their fakes than any of their *bona-fide* colleagues. Slightly related to this class are artists such as Marochetti (100): capable *costumiers* who distinguish themselves from forgers primarily by not creating their sculptures with fraudulent intent but who, nevertheless, try to furnish the collector with sculptures that are as close as possible to the already familar work of Renaissance and Baroque sculptors.

At this point, one must consider the most specifically nineteenth-century

★ The small bronze of the Renaissance, although extremely popular and produced in large quantities, was never the major goal of sculpture in the *quattro* and *cinquecento*. It was either a by-product of a master whose main work was the creation of monumental statuary or else it was the staple product of a lesser artist who, following the major trends of art determined by his superiors, created in his smaller bronzes a more diffused divulgation of the style of monumental sculpture. More important still, the Renaissance bronze is infinitely more committed, bears a strong charge of a very precise artistic volition and is, in general, dedicated to resuscitating the harmony and beauty of antiquity. The so-called art-bronze is far more detached and, though technically impeccable, it does not carry conviction of the concentrated, strained energies of artistic creation. A decorative laxness of form is evident in almost all this production.

An interesting sidelight on nineteenth-century sculptural tastes is shed by the history of collecting. The Renaissance or Baroque bronze which during the eighteenth century became a vitrine-curio, a *Luxuskabinettstück*, was reinstated in the nineteenth century as a high form of independent art . . . which it rarely was even at the time of its inception. Rodin is the one who clarifies the meaning of Renaissance bronzes and the French art-bronze. It is very possible that *The old courtesan* (118) was inspired by a Riccio bronze representing an old, naked witch. The Riccio (iii), in its correctly diminutive size, is meant as a curiosity. Rodin, elevating the theme from the freakishness it held for Riccio, also enlarges the size of his sculpture to a far more monumental format.

phenomenon in sculpture: the spurious artist or, as Baudelaire was to call him, the *pompier*. Unique in the history of art, he must not be confused with the third-rate artist of previous epochs. This latter category is always recognized as such by contemporaries, and serves to introduce on a large scale the style of recognized masters to a broader public. The inferior artist of the Baroque or the Renaissance inserts himself easily into the general scheme by following in the footsteps of an artist greater than himself. Though he may now and then hit on fortunate and personal solutions, he never sets the style. One can, at a pinch, disregard him, without seriously distorting one's understanding of the epoch in which he was operative.

The nineteenth-century or our own contemporary *pompier*, on the other hand, is much more representative of the taste and culture of his day than is the dedicated artist who works in obscurity. We today may appreciate Barye, Préault and Daumier far more than we do Clésinger or Pradier. Yet it is this latter group of artists who set the general tone of sculpture, who fully represented the dominating cultural taste of their time, and not the former three, who were working counter-current. If we base our idea of the nineteenth century on the masters whom we recognize as great today we shall fail to understand the nineteenth century. And we shall also fail to understand Barye and Daumier. If we are to gauge their full grandeur it is essential that we know what and whom they were struggling against. For the seventeenth century, we can look to Bernini or to some minor *atelier* assistant without being led astray about the nature of Baroque taste. There is a coherence here that, in the nineteenth century, vanishes without trace. Nothing but antagonism relates Daumier to his officially praised colleagues.

Because there was no market for him, the *pompier* had never existed before, except in Holland after 1650, where similar processes of secularization and mercantilism created a situation akin to that of the nineteenth century. With very few exceptions the commissioner of sculpture had been on a cultural par with the sculptor, and could, therefore, choose with discrimination. The unrecognized or neglected artist of great talent did not really exist before the French Revolution because his contemporaries were too well trained, too much aware of the importance of finding the right artist, not to recognize his talent. Such important exceptions as Puget and, to some degree, Michelangelo depend more on the morbid inclinations of the artist than on the lack of recognition.

The *pompier*, then, was usually a competent craftsman who met his public half way by ministering to their wishes. Unlike the true artist, he was not concerned with the truth of his talent or the validity of his conceptions. On

iii Attributed to ANDREA RICCIO
Padua 1470–1532
Old woman seated bronze
Paris, Bibliothèque Nationale

command, he would furnish funerary sculpture showing the survival of the soul, even though he himself might not believe in resurrection; he would supply allegories without believing in the existence of a transcendental world in which the qualities he celebrated were ideally incorporated in human shape. He would carefully avoid mentioning themes which, though fundamental to his times, might offend his commissioners: the rise of the proletariat, the brutalization of the masses, the irrelevance of individual destiny in a secularized world which insisted on the here and now, and had little admiration for the beyond. And he would generally express himself in a style which depended on two factors, both of them dear to the heart of the broad public: reference to the classical past by means of the idealization of forms, and a strict adherence to journalistically correct description of reality which even the most naïve eye could comprehend at a glance. Such a style, naturally, is good for all occasions. It can, and often does, immortalize the most antagonistic ideals. In our century, Communists and Fascists, democratic and totalitarian governments have set monuments to their heroes and to their ideological concepts which are practically identical in style.

All of the conditions, symptoms and problems which gathered density and came to a climax towards the end of the nineteenth century were already visible in Neoclassicism. Though, superficially, the style of Canova and Thorvaldsen seems reactionary and backward-looking, it is, in fact, prophetic. In many ways Canova is closer to Brancusi than he is to Bernini or Falconet.

Neoclassicism is distinguished from all previous Classic styles and renaissances by being a style to which nostalgia is a *sine qua non*. During the Carolingian and the Florentine Renaissance, and in France in the seventeenth century, there were endeavours to re-create the glories of a vanished past. Neoclassicism, paradoxically at the very time when Pompeii and Herculaneum offered more information about antiquity than had ever existed before, depended on a romantic yearning for a golden age which could never be reconstituted. It is significant that the antiquities preferred by Canova (e.g. the Spada reliefs) belong to a period which was itself nostalgic for the fifth century B.C.

The first stage of Neoclassicism was marked by an easy harmony with Rococo theatricalism. One played at living in the antique mode as one played at being a milk-maid; and it is significant that these two theatrical *genres* were often interwoven. The pastoral theme of make-believe at Le Hameau (iv) was directly related to the bucolic life which derived from Theocritan ideals.

This phase was also accompanied by the rise of the middle classes in France and England, which were avidly in search of a style that would express their culture as distinct from the culture of the Court. It was given a special impulse by the needs of mass manufacturers such as Josiah Wedgwood. Wedgwood found in Neoclassicism an ideal style for his pottery; it combined great prestige with practicability, since Classicism, unlike the more spontaneously personal Rococo style, could be taught to generations of new apprentices. Furthermore, the Classical style, embodying middle-class ideals of rationalism and political liberty, rapidly became a polemic style, expressing the demands which were being formulated at the same time by the rising power of the *bourgeoisie*.

The attitude towards the Classic past is, throughout, a very complex one. Primarily it is romantic. The spectral resurrection of buried cities has all the fascination of a ghost rising from the grave. One must remember that visits to Pompeii and Herculaneum were undertaken by torchlight, just as the great collections of antiquities were also visited at night with artificial illumination: this was the custom at the Court of Sweden, for instance, and is also the method recommended by Goethe.

Yet, at the same time, quite soberly and without the romantic posturing of travellers worshipping in the Vesuvian cities, archaeology was born. History was turned into a science, and ceased to be a speculation on the mysterious way of God; it became a scientific process in which all sorts of evidence must be assembled, arranged and interpreted. The lowly implements brought to light at Pompeii, the casual items of daily use, now became as important as the most sublime paintings and sculptures. The hierarchy of values which obtained before were now broken down. Once the hierarchic structure of values is shaken, once objects become important for the clues which they yield up instead of for their beauty or their manifestation of faith, one object is equivalent to another, and the artist is faced with a situation in which it does not matter whether he paints flowers or a face. For the sculptor especially this state of affairs is important. Eventually, with Duchamp, we witness the ultimate consequences of this nascent rupture in the hierarchic order of things: a mass-produced object (258), rather than its man-produced mimic, is chosen to be a sculpture in its own right simply because it has a tremendous charge of archaeological meaning about the time in which it was manufactured. And, as such, it has more meaning than the reproduction of a thing in nature since, considered from the rationalistic, secularized point of view of the times, a still-life is as important or as irrelevant as the figure of a saint. The decisive difference lies in the act of perception of

IV PIERRE JULIEN
b. Saint-Paulien 1731 – d. Paris 1804
Amalthea 1791
Rambouillet, Laiterie de la Reine

value . . . not in an inherent, native value conferred on an object by its God-willed place in the universe.

This break in traditional relationships, which depended previously on a commonly shared belief in the centrality of God who represented the supreme value which diminished the further one left God behind, is also noticeable in the curious fragmentation of composition. Each figure seems to exist in its own right and no longer interacts dramatically or visually with its companions. Only when he returns to his Rococo origins does Canova fuse his figures in expressive, inclusive compositions, e.g. *Cupid and Psyche* (4) which was criticized by Neoclassic theoreticians in Germany for being a *moulin à vent rococo.* In his Classic vein, e.g. *Tomb of Maria Christina* (10), figures move without being aware of each other in a manner which already predicts, given the wisdom of hindsight, Giacometti (282).

But, primarily, it is the different attitude towards the subject which makes of Neoclassicism the first modern style in sculpture. And this aspect reveals itself most clearly in the very appearance of the sculptures. Encountering Bernini's *Apollo and Daphne* (v) in the Galleria Borghese, Rome, one's first, immediate reaction is the recognition of Apollo and Daphne or, if one lacks the Classical training for such a recognition, one directly recognizes a fleeing female being embraced by a pursuing male. It is only after a more prolonged viewing that one comes to admire Bernini's manipulation of textures, composition and gestures, which have conspired to make one first see a convincing, breathtaking incarnation of the artist's vision and later, by means of a wilful, more intellectual examination, to admire the method by which the artist has achieved his goal.

Stepping from the Bernini sculpture to Canova's *Paolina Borghese* (12) in the same museum, the process is inverted. What one is shaken by first is the unutterably strong appeal of the stone and its magnificent cutting. The cool, aloof harmony of outlines and masses, the varying transparencies and densities, these speak to us at the outset. Only then do we go on to be impressed by the subject and its interpretation. No one could ever be tempted to mistake this superlative, icy effigy for a woman in the same way that we *are* tempted at first glance to see Daphne rushing towards us as she tries to escape Apollo's embrace. The material, even mechanical look of modern sculpture which sometimes bursts out in grotesque but significant episodes, such as the lawsuit brought by the United States Customs Authorities against Brancusi for trying to import a manufactured article (191), is one of the most important characteristics of modern sculpture, and persists to our day. The drama of sculpture before our modern epoch lies in the victory which the artist wins in his effort to overcome the dull, inert resistance of his lifeless material. And the great artist never lets the question of 'How did he do it?' arise. Whether we look at the Royal Portal at Chartres or at Bernini's *St Theresa*, it is the victory of mind over matter which impresses us first and last.

In modern sculpture the accent is put on the battle itself. With the material world having become aggressive under the impulses it receives from mechanization and secularization so that sheer matter steadily grows to dominate rather than serve man, the artist has to struggle harder, and must rely on his own resources since all traditional weapons fail him in this novel situation. The artist, be he Rodin, Canova, Brancusi or the latest Pop Artist,

I Antonio Canova
Meekness (Mansuetudine) 1783
Possagno, Gipsoteca Canovian

II Jean-Baptiste Carpeaux
Neapolitan fisherboy 1863
Washington, D.C.
National Gallery of Art
Samuel H. Kress Collection

III Auguste Rodin
La Défense 1878
Paris, Musée Rodin
(II & III *overleaf*)

demands of us a double and simultaneous vision: he asks us to be aware of the tough resistance which his material exerts and to watch his struggle to circumvent and defeat it. The outcome of the struggle is often irrelevant. It is the heroic will to find his own way despite all opposition, it is the artist's determination to force order, answers, secrets from his material which really matters. This attitude becomes especially explicit in Rodin who deliberately poses all the tactical phases of the battle by going from brute mass to the highest finish in one and the same sculpture. The comparison with Michelangelo is meaningless here. Michelangelo, either through circumstance or personal inclination, left many statues incomplete. The implication of each one, however, was that it *could* be completed. The very essence of Rodin's work, however, is that it can *not* be completed in the traditional way, but exists only by reason of its fluctuating struggle in which the ultimate decision must remain ambiguous.

The same holds true of the most diverse artists such as Brancusi, Picasso, Duchamp or Lipchitz. True, Brancusi aims at conveying states of existence which are completely intangible; but the vehicle he chooses is always of the most concretely physical nature: roughly hewn wood, brass polished to an uncanny, mechanical lustre, marble which is cut in such a way as to retain all the characteristics of the natural state of the stone. It is here that Canova reveals himself as closer to his followers than to his ancestors. Whereas Bernini polished his stone to evoke the sensation of skin or hair, Canova polishes his stone in order to bring out the beauty of the stone and not of the skin or hair which it is made to represent. The choice of material is revealing, too. The translucent, even-grained alabaster preferred by Canova is far more assertive than the denser, crystalline yellowish marble chosen by Bernini.

The ambiguities and complexities of Canova's work and life are infinite, but at least one more aspect must preoccupy us: the homelessness of modern sculpture. Where, for instance, does *Paolina Borghese* belong? Or where, for that matter, should one place the colossal statue of her brother, *Napoleon* (11)? If one recognizes the figure as Napoleon, then his nudity out in a public square becomes all too personal and embarrassing. If one does not recognize Napoleon, but sees instead an anonymous antique hero-god, then the statue fails in its purpose. Apparently aware of the dilemma, Canova decided to build a pantheon in his native village of Possagno, a neutral ground, in which his works could be assembled. More than half a century later, in 1880, Rodin was to create an ideal, neutral home for his sculptures in *The gates of Hell* (120), which deliberately sunders itself from any architectural or practical

IV Edgar Degas
The little ballet-dancer,
14 years old 1880
London, Tate Gallery

25

V GIOVANNI-LORENZO BERNINI
b. Naples 1598 – d. Rome, 1680
Apollo and Daphne 1622
Rome, Galleria Borghese

function; and more recently still, Brancusi donated his sculptures to the French State, provided they kept his studio intact, because only in this setting were the sculptures really at home. Generally, our modern experience of modern sculpture comes to us not in the healthy, natural manner of things which belong to our daily lives, but through visits to museums, artificial no-man's land – or everyman's land, which amounts to the same thing. The number of sculptures which insert themselves fluently into normal civic existence is extremely restricted. One thinks of Carpeaux's *The dance* (92), Rodin's *Balzac* (130) and hopes that the courageous experiments of cities like Rotterdam, Antwerp and St Gallen in acquiring sculpture for urban decoration (110, 236, 336, 338), will be successfully imitated in non-provincial centres.

★   ★   ★

Romanticism is not as easily definable in sculpture as is Neoclassicism, because it is such an integral factor, both in preceding as well as subsequent styles. Without Romantic elements, Neoclassicism is unthinkable just as Realistic sculpture and Rodin are impossible without the participation of the Romantic experience.

In Pinelli (44) we see the confluence of Classic (his proud claim to be a true son of Rome), Romantic (his love of the picturesque and emotionally charged subject), and Realistic attitudes (his determination to render observed scenes with stringent realism) flow inextricably together. In Bartolini (48) and de Fauveau (66), the former proud of being a Classicist, the latter an inflammatory Romanticist, we can observe the consequences of Neoclassicism's archaeological, historical attributes. Once antiquity was posed as the unattainable ideal, it followed quite logically that other Classical epochs, especially the Florentine Renaissance as well as pre-Classical periods which fathered Classicism, should draw the attention of artists.

Perhaps the purest expression of Romanticism in sculpture is to be found in the work of Préault (63–5, 67). Explosively arbitrary in choice of subjects, defying all previous concepts of finish, composition, coherence and comprehensibility, he is by far the most important ancestor of Rodin and all subsequent developments in art, including Cubism (his fragmentation of form, his proposition that forms can be discontinuous) and Surrealism (his uncanny power to evoke hallucinatory states of mind). There is also his reaction against the rationale of Classicism in his passionate return to religious subjects, and a sardonic, demoniac humour which associates him with Byronic heroes with whom he also shares disdain for the overripe, tempting, ruinous city-civilization and often shows signs of yearning for the rude purity of peasant life. But Préault, the greatest and least-known sculptor in France before Rodin, remains an isolated exception. Romanticism with its emotional effects, instability of form and stormy passions is not congruent with the stability and the limited colour-range of sculpture.

More instructive of the ambiguities of Romanticism is the confrontation of Barye and Daumier. The former was extolled by Delacroix as the greatest of Romantic sculptors, and certainly his themes of savagery and uncontrolled animal force, which he rendered with unrivalled, galvanic enthusiasm, belong to the Romantic repertory. Yet his anatomical studies, carried out in the dissection room, his interminable studies in front of the cages in the Jardin des Plantes, have all the progressive features of programmatic, anti-romantic Realism. Daumier, the most ardent exponent of Realism in his political cartoons and in his paintings, involved heart and soul with the lot of the defeated and exploited and courageously avoiding all temptations of the exotic, created sculptures of such spirit, of such passionate, intuitive force, overcoming all dictates of visual perception, that he ought properly to be catalogued with the Romanticists. The truth is that sculpture does not keep step with painting. The categories which have been used to more or less good advantage in the much more closely studied and familiar field of nineteenth-century painting do not hold true for sculpture which, more thoroughly disorientated by the new conditions, took far longer to recover than painting did.

In sculpture Romanticism's major contribution consists of the enormously enlarged scope of subjects, the flexibility of composition and the introduction of unorthodox materials. The irrational motivations of art are now taken into consideration, especially in Préault's work, and, most important of all, a new place is assigned to the ugly as a viable theme for the artist.

Not that ugliness did not exist before Romanticism. But, generally speaking, it existed either as a virtuoso freak designed to single out the artist's talent for observation and precision of technique or else it existed, as, for instance, in the work of Rembrandt, who is reinstated as one of the great artists of all time by the Romanticists, as the tragic counterbalance to spiritual refinement. Especially the early stages of Romanticism are full of experiments with essentially ugly subject-matter. Again, Pinelli can serve as an example. *The wounded brigand* (44) is almost certainly inspired by South Italian *presepio* figurines (vi). These *presepio* carvings were eminently realistic in intention and execution, and quite free from the theatrical and picturesque qualities of contemporary prettified porcelain vagabonds. But in the *presepio*, a stubborn

vi GIUSEPPE SAMMARTINO
Naples 1723–93
The shepherd
Naples, Museo Nazionale

28

and almost journalistic reportage of rude, unwashed humanity, was the necessary polarity to the divine, ineffably beautiful event of the Nativity; it is the tribute mortal man offers to an eternally and supremely beautiful sanctity. Ugliness is made to serve moralizing purposes because it teaches that in the rude exterior there may lurk a heart susceptible to worshipping the Christ Child. Pinelli retains the full-blooded realism of the *presepio* but does not endow it with any nobler purpose. Ugliness is simply a condition of modern man. His deeds and his appearance are not capable any longer of interpretation into transcendental terms. This acceptance of the factual, indestructible nature of appearance can also be discovered in Rude's *Tomb of Godefroi de Cavaignac* (61), and in Barye's struggling animals, whose ferocity serves no higher purpose but reveals a blind force in nature which is a law unto itself and which is not susceptible to ennoblement.

Carpeaux's work represents the first attempt at healing the fateful divorce between official and non-official art. Endowed with unusual strength of talent, and capable of freeing himself from aesthetic programmes, he is a forerunner of Rodin not only stylistically, but also in his intentions of bringing a new unity of expression and of style to the art of sculpture. His earliest successful piece, *Ugolino and his children* (87), already shows the freedom of conception, the monumentality of composition and the powerful devotion to observed truth that make a comparison with Rodin's *The thinker* (see *The gates of Hell* (120)) quite plausible. On his return from Rome, he was attacked by the Academy for being too vulgarly close to natural appearance. However, the political situation was propitious for a young sculptor of bold new talent, and he was sponsored by the Court of Napoleon III who was eager to exert his power over cultural affairs, and sought to lessen the monopoly of the Academy. Returning for the first time since the Revolution to the sensibility and freshness of execution characteristic of the great eighteenth-century French sculptors, Carpeaux achieved a deftness of portraiture, a precision and a spontaneity of subtle modelling such as had not been seen for half a century. Nor is his art, though it tends towards the attractive, ever trifling. Modulations, expressions, gestures and decorative additions, costumes, flowers and so on, are always carefully adjusted to the ultimate impression and meaning of his work. Unlike most of his contemporaries, he knew the enormous importance of the void. The shape, swing and rhythms of his voids are as carefully composed as are the volumes which they separate. It seems almost impossible today that his *chef-d'œuvre, The dance* (92), the most exuberantly optimistic sculptural statement of the entire century, should have been attacked for its alleged indecency; and we can gauge the degree of

29

hypocritical prudery rampant even in Paris by the fact that an attempt was made to deface the monument.

Rodin, though of infinitely greater variety, inventiveness and scope, and though his field is the tragic lot of man, is not a negation of Carpeaux but rather an enlargement. He too has the ambition of filling the gap which had deepened between the official and the non-official. His ambition was to assert himself in public, not to withdraw into an independent world. In his work, as in the work of preceding sculptors, there remains a certain cleavage between his 'private' and his 'public' works, but it is a division he always sought to overcome and, after he had successfully established himself, he never hesitated to risk all that he had achieved in order to propagate his personal vision, heedless of the outrage it might provoke among the public.

Rodin has often been classed with the Impressionists, but the comparison is vain. Impressionism strives against moral, historical, emotional commitment on the part of the artist. Landscape and still-life are its primary *genres* and even figures are treated as if they were still-lifes or elements of a landscape. Rodin, on the contrary, rebelling against all the excesses of drapery, decorative elements and so on, of popular Academic portrait sculpture, returned to the human body as his central theme and never used the body but to force from it some vital, hitherto unexpressed, secret of the human soul.

Only in one respect, and it is a tenuous one, does the work of Rodin resemble Impressionism. To the Impressionists, the known, perceived world is mutable in direct ratio to the light which illuminates it. A painting, therefore, is finished when the light changes. Now Rodin's sculptures, though they do gain tremendous vitality from their vivid, light-catching surfaces, do not depend on light. But the suggestion, in all of his work, that forms are never integral, but always in the state of becoming something else, does create a binding link with the painting of a Monet or a Pissarro. It is not a stable, climactic moment which the artist has caught and fixed, nor is it the equally stable moment just before the climax, the moment of suspense so dear to Baroque artists, that interests Rodin. It is rather the non-existence of moments, the continuity of time without breaks, climaxes or pauses which inspires him. Nobody has ever more fully and clearly expressed than he the eroding, irresistible action of time which perpetually threatens us.

Cubism, taking up suggestions from Rodin, has investigated time and its action within space more analytically and more in keeping with the changed, scientifically known universe in which we live. But, though Cubism may have graphed movement and timed the passage of objects through space, it has never been able to achieve what Rodin achieved: to represent the passage of time in all its tragic extent as a condition of human existence, to evaluate the eternal human hope for moral stability in a perpetually fluctuating world. The heroic gesture of self-sacrifice of *The burghers of Calais* (127–9), for instance, is not presented as such but is shown against the foreknowledge that even the most heroic acts of self-abnegation will in time be forgotten and cancelled from human memory. It is this conviction that the tragic, but imperative, duty of the sculptor is to raise monuments to humanity which gives each of his figures a tragic sonority, not only in its subject and content but in its very form, a form which is fugitive and suggestive of several strata of contradictory, antagonistic meaning.

Rodin is also the only sculptor of his time who derives his strength not from a detached, purely personal inspiration, but from a full understanding of the human condition at a particular moment in history. He disdains to gloss over and he scorns to turn away from important aspects of modern existence. He either battles with them directly or discovers new possibilities of self-knowledge. Thus, from the irrevocable loss of individualization in a materialistic, secularized world, which grinds away the personal, he draws new conclusions and benefits. The weakened dictates of physiognomic resemblance allow him to go directly to the irreducible germ of human existence without having to pause to record the features of a face. Hundreds of his statues and statuettes have no heads or no faces. Yet each one reveals itself fully because the artist knew how to strike directly to the very heart of individuality. There he is in direct contrast with Degas, who, even when he minutely records the smallest details of a face, deliberately cancels out any hope for meaningful individuality, for meaningful life, by making the sum of his details equal zero.

The fragmentation and the isolation which we already noticed in the works of Canova become conscious in Rodin, and are incorporated into his scheme of relationships. Groups, even when embracing, are about to be sundered; and grouping in the traditional manner of geometric configuration, which was introduced by the Renaissance, usually is completely suppressed or exploded. In *The burghers of Calais* the grouping is deliberately disjointed to demonstrate the isolation of each man's agony; and only the presentiment of a common death against which each struggles in his own way holds them together. But in the groups which crown *The gates of Hell* (120), the coming together of the figures results from an immense outside pressure, which, once released, will have the opposite effect of dispersing figures accidentally brought together by forces outside themselves. Even in the

vii GASPARD PUGET
    Near Marseilles 1620–94
    Milo of Crotone 1683
    Paris, Louvre

most explosive Baroque groups, by Puget or Adam, for instance, admired by Rodin, the massing, though it may be antagonistic, nevertheless resolves itself into a stable form derived from the inner action of the figure. It is impossible to imagine Puget's *Milo of Crotone* (vii) as changing his position or without the tree-trunk or the lion. *The three shades* or any other Rodin group *can* be taken apart, and often was, by Rodin himself. Their interrelationship does not depend on an interior logic which binds them into a predestined enduring whole, as is the case even with Puget, but each figure, being in itself a fragment, cannot build up to anything but an even larger fragment, which is sustained only by the compelling, often arbitrary will of the artists who reserve the right to disperse the composition at any time. In that respect *The gates of Hell*, never finished, never capable of being finished, spewing forth figures, swallowing them up again like a tomb, is the most perfectly realized of all of Rodin's works.

★   ★   ★

The plates of this volume include a great deal of aesthetically invalid material which demands explanation. The preceding pages have attempted to trace the course of the major, the melodic development of nineteenth-century sculpture. But, as has been demonstrated, the Academic *basso continuo* which accompanies the work of the few great masters is the predominant tone, and must be discussed at great length.

Perhaps the greatest strength of the academic-official style of sculpture is the inherent weakness of its opponents. For Romanticism, by stressing the personal, the unique and the exotic, by favouring, in short, a revolutionary attitude on the part of the artist, not only alienates the sculpture-commissioning public but also deprives the Romantic school of a coherent continuity. By the time the public has become familiar with, and benevolent to, one development of Romantic expression, the next generation of revolutionary artists has appeared on the scene to shock a basically sluggish public. Classicism, since it depends on verbally communicable, stable principles is slow to change and therefore appeals to the public which prefers the familiar.

The teachability of Classicism as well as its prestige makes it extremely adaptable for the market. In an era of mass-production and of rapid consumption on the part of a vastly increased buying public, sculpture, reduced to the level of merchandise by losing its traditional commissioners among the aristocracy and the Church, must keep pace by adapting itself. And again it is the Classic mode which answers the demand of such important sectors of the market as funeral sculpture because a man with some academic training, directing a large workshop, can supervise the production of large numbers of statuary which is executed not by him but by a regiment of stone-cutters. The Romantic independent sculptor cannot possibly compete since his work depends on personal finish, original inventions and the unteachable element of a mysterious moment of inspiration.

The Academic procedure as such has its origins in Thorvaldsen rather than in Canova. Canova's vigorous peasant-like love of sensuous reality, the lust for manipulating clay or wax, his craftsman's admiration of good workmanship, always hold the balance to theory and prevent theory from becoming all-important. Even if he did not necessarily cut the stones himself, he most attentively followed and directed the final carving, and the sly but healthy regard he has for the attractions of the female figure are indication enough of the care he lavished on the finished marble.

By contrast Thorvaldsen is far more anonymous in his treatment of surfaces and masses. The perfection of a composition, the utmost clarity of design, the scrupulous exclusion of private, idiosyncratic emotional responses make the sheerly sensuous appearance of his sculptures a matter of indifference. One is often tempted to caress a Canova, but rarely does one care to come too close to a Thorvaldsen, whose even surfaces and slightly flaccid volumes never appeal to a muscular, haptic or visceral response on the part of the spectator.

This anonymity of appearance and style that is characteristic of Academic sculpture is paralleled by a peculiar neutrality in the subject-matter. Since personal interpretation and emotional response was derided by the Academic artist, he naturally tended to keep his subject-matter very low in tone. Generalized allegories were designed where the meaning did not depend on their plausible incarnation of a given virtue (e.g. Bernini's *Charity* is unmistakable even if one does not understand the attributes of the figure); rather they were blank forms which could be filled with meanings depending on the occasion by simply adding diverse attributes suitable to the desired significance. Allegory became heraldic rather than immediate. Thorvaldsen's angels (14), for example, and saints, are not necessarily recognizable as higher, celestial beings.

Since the Academic traditions quickly degenerate into a mere correctness of formulations, accentuating the tasteful, or, at least, the exclusion of the tasteless, rather than the original, the execution soon becomes a matter of supreme indifference to both the public and the artists. True, a certain division of labour has always existed in sculptural *ateliers*, and Bernini undoubtedly relied on a number of assistants to help him in the carving and polishing of his statues. Yet the presence of the master dominated every step from conception to completion. Now, among official creators of statuary, the actual artist is sometimes very hard to find. The *Monument to the completion of the Fréjus Tunnel* in Turin (109), for instance, was conceived by Panissera who described his general idea to Belli. Belli then made a vague model in clay which was given more precise definition by the students of the local academy in a gesso model. This model was then turned over to a commercial stone-cutting firm which constructed the monument itself. Who is the artist?

★   ★   ★

The advantage of Classicism, its cohesive continuity, brings with it a detrimental element: boredom. The general public, even though it prefers the familiar to the shockingly novel, will, in the end, lose interest in sculpture altogether if it is not stimulated by certain tricks which will give outworn formulation a spurious air of originality. It is fateful and noteworthy that Academicism, when it comes to realize its own deficiencies and tries to remedy them by borrowing from Romanticism, inevitably borrows not the germ of Romanticism's vitality but the germ of Romanticism's death: the nervous hunting for novelty at any cost.

To offset the danger of boredom, then, Academicism has recourse to giganticism and spectacular setting. Again Thorvaldsen is the beginning of an enormous development. His *Lion of Lucerne* (16), with its huge dimensions and in its ravishing setting, is the ancestor of a number of public monuments too large to survey.

The crisis of Academicism towards the last quarter of the century becomes quite evident to the official artists themselves. Bartholdi is perhaps the most conscious and intelligent artist in that respect, and successfully staves off the inevitable bankruptcy for several decades by a technical brilliance which is unjustly ignored or derided today. That he was quite clear in his own mind about the state of official sculpture appears from the correspondence between the sculptor and the Mayor of Belfort concerning the erection of a monument commemorating the heroic defence of that city during the Franco-Prussian War. Bartholdi, trying to win the mayor over to his conception of the monument, states quite baldly that any statue placed in a public square or park of the city would be irrelevant to the particular sacrifice made by the citizens of Belfort, since the same monument could just as easily be moved to any other city. Instead, he suggests that a megalomaniac lion, conventional symbol of bravery, be carved into the red-stone bluffs which overlook and dominate the city (101). Thus, the monument will truly belong to Belfort and remind all who visit the city of its courage during the war. The implications are obvious: no statue can, by itself, be relevant to the anonymous heroism of Belfort's citizenry. Sculpture has lost its contact with the lives and deaths of men. Only the setting, the native stone and the brute dimensions of the monument can express the extent of the sacrifice and suggest the locale in which this sacrifice was offered.

★   ★   ★

By compelling the official art world to recognize his genius, and by bringing together all that is most viable in the very concept of tradition and the revolutionary ardour of Romanticism, Rodin radically changed the situation. The Academy, in recognizing him, confessed its own bankruptcy . . . but, by so doing, saved itself from ruin, and quickly floated new credits by assimilating the appearance of Rodin's work without penetrating to the interior necessities which led Rodin to discover and give meaning to his revolutionary concepts. What was fiery exclamation in Rodin was converted into bombastic rhetoric. Fragmentation which in Rodin conveyed a definite statement pertaining to man's estate became licence to leave work unfinished.

The reaction against Rodin's dispersion of sculptural mass, which was first given full form by Maillol, also came to the rescue of an Academicism which felt itself to be at bay. Without heeding the extremely personal reinterpretation of Greek Severe Style sculpture, official sculptors seized on Maillol's noble simplicity as a harbinger of a return to the bland and non-committal Classicism of the mid-nineteenth century.

In the same way an incredibly tenacious Academic strain, kept alive primarily by public funds, absorbed Primitive art, first discovered by Gauguin, Matisse and Picasso, who drew from it very personal and aesthetically important conclusions which acted as a fructifying force in their own work. Thus almost every conceivable folk-idiom from Viking to Japanese to Navajo was exploited without the least regard for the integrity of style. Generally a high polish, attractive for itself but also because it proved that the artist had worked hard, accompanies this kind of sculptural decoration as does a giganticism which staggers the imagination.

The most radical and the most fascinating expression of official art, and also the most complete record of what happens when government and artists co-operate to create, programmatically, with malice aforethought, is furnished us by the Fascist style which gathered such momentum during the twenties and thirties of our century that it can be called an international style. Wherever governments during this time decided on publicly sponsored sculptural or architectural complexes, a powerful affinity with the Fascist style made itself felt, even though the form of government differed from country to country.

The Fascist experience is even more interesting to the historian of modern sculpture, because it began not with a tradition-bound academy but with one of the most revolutionary of modern art movements: Futurism. In this respect, as well as in many others, the art-propaganda of Fascist Italy was infinitely more insidious, infinitely more intelligent and infinitely more experimental than its German counterpart. It accepted the fact that Futurism was the first Italian style since Canova's Classicism which had universal European currency, and seized on it as its most powerful vehicle of cultural propaganda. The original members of the Futurist movement, had they survived the war, would have been horrified at the use that was being made of their theories. For, despite the aggressive bombast of Futurist manifestoes, their political concepts were naïve and purposeless, designed to shock an apathetic, hopelessly provincial country into an awareness of what had been happening in the world's capitals.

Carefully vitiating all those basic principles of Futurism which spoke for the right of the artist to propose new visions of the world and of man, Fascism kept intact only the magnificent, surging form of Futurist sculpture, and having once assured itself of possession of an admired and admirable contemporary style slowly distorted it towards its own propagandistic needs. The overwrought rhetoric, the boasting, the promises of a new golden age were easily equated with the powerful energies which Futurist sculptors had infused into their works. But since the naked, abstract presentation of mechanical forces was not necessarily understandable to the masses, Futurist abstraction, derived from an anthropocentric style which it then destroyed, was once again put back into its old bottle: the human figure. Only now the human figure was agitated by an extravagant muscularity, a brutal onslaught of blind power, which had its origin in no single emotion, but was simply an attribute of the animal nature of the human frame. The petrified fury which shakes the figures of Fascist monuments is the most graphic illustration of the regimentation which the country suffered to be imposed on it. Armies with nowhere to go, energies which are hurled against no visible enemy, the whole waste and senselessness of the Fascist programme is inherent in these sculptures, which are as fascinating as they are repulsive but which also express a national state of mind with an uncanny precision and must therefore be reckoned with when final accounts of our century's sculpture are set up. The victory of the *pompier* in every phase and particle of human existence is symbolized here, and certainly this victory of arrogance is one of the most anguishing and most important problems of our time. Surrealists and other serious sculptors as well have tried to present and clarify this horrifying process of brutalization, which makes itself continually more felt in our lives. But their work, by attaining the clarity and detachment of art, is at a disadvantage when compared with the work of the *pompier*. The artist's work contains values and an affirmation in the act of human creation which cancels out the destructive forces predominating in our day. The *pompier*'s work, since it offers no catharsis, is more directly frightening, more immediately eloquent of all that we fear most.

De Chirico, when he first painted his pictures of Italian city squares with their nineteenth-century equestrian monuments, pointed to an unexpected, paradoxical possibility: perhaps the Academic art, the art of the *pompier*, is the only possible folk-art of the past century and a half. For, seen in retrospect, when these sculptures have lost the arrogance of political situations which they were meant to celebrate, they have a peculiarly fragile air, despite all their ostensible assurance and solidity. Now that the myths of a usurped and propagandistic glory have been exploded, what is more touching than the trumpeting charge of sculptures on the *Monument to Victor Emmanuel II* (159)? These sculptures, which in their hypocrisy and outworn declamatory style once irritated the sensitive among our forebears, now appear like a whimsical *memento mori* and gain a certain apposite expressiveness. Though they were meant to commemorate a vainglorious national exaltation, a duty for which they were ill-suited, they now attain a certain fitness as the memorial for a world which deluded itself and met its fate because of its treacherous pseudo-ideals.

★　　★　　★

Considering that we are only today and only very gradually beginning to achieve enough distance from the work of nineteenth-century sculptors in order to arrive at a dispassionate and stable evaluation of their work, the confusion and antagonism which must necessarily arise from any survey of the sculpture of our own day will come as no surprise. Hampered by lack of perspective and faced with a multiplicity of contemporaneous styles such as the world has never seen before, today's critic is bound to disturb a large segment of his public by omissions or by negative judgements. With the possible exception of Brancusi, we have no established old masters who can be used as a standard. Even the most celebrated reputations of today await the inevitable process of rejection and rediscovery before a detached, relatively accurate estimate of their worth can be distilled in some future evaluation. As it stands now, we lack even a suitable idiom for dealing with modern sculptural concepts and have to fall back on that used for painting. Thus Cubism, when used in relation to painting, has a very definite meaning and covers a clearly defined quantity of works. The same word when applied to sculpture becomes far more elusive. During the Fauvist, Expressionist and Cubist periods sculpture was an ancillary to painting, developing at a much more irregular pace both chronologically and qualitatively. Today's sculptor is infinitely more reticent than his painter-colleague. He is also considerably more reluctant to band together with others and seems unwilling to accept the verdicts and assessments of critics.

For all these reasons, today's sculpture is probably a healthier and more independent art than painting, but its creators have not been able to conquer the public imagination with the same vigour and brilliance with which modern painters impose taste on vast segments of the public. The illustrations in this book, as well as the following text, can make no claim to being 'a guide' to modern sculpture. They offer, at best, a path that has been hacked in the jungle. Even a simple chronology presents serious problems. Originality and pure inventiveness have become far more prized than genuine talent, and very often even the best of artists has contradicted himself in order to gain a point in the game of precedence. When Picasso said '*L'art nègre?* . . . *Connais pas!*' he actually did more than try to claim for himself alone the discovery of a new formal freedom. He also waged war against the type of criticism which wants nothing but clear-cut lines of influence and an easy progression from one 'ism' to the next. Perhaps a little confusion is not too high a price to pay for a survey of the enormous variety of modern sculpture. Logical coherence has never been the most notable attribute of progress in the arts.

Modern sculpture after Rodin is an exploratory art. The Romantic urge to return to fundamentals is still very strong. Rodin, by breaking through to a concept of sculpture which no longer depended on an unchangeable mass, laid bare a wealth of possibilities which are still being investigated today. Another concomitant of Rodin's art – the will to integrate sculpture with everyday life, to range sculpture with all that is born, lives and dies, as against earlier timeless sculpture, carved to stem the tide of encroaching time by eternalizing and monumentalizing a single moment – has given rise to an ever greater concentration on the natural aspects of sculpture. Mass and void, surface and inner bulk, the 'lump and the hole', the reaction of these aspects to gravity and relation to the field of interaction, which are set up as soon as an autonomous shape is thrust into juxtaposition with an amorphous environment, are current features of modern sculpture.

Gauguin's flight from Europe and the totemic idols he carved in Tahiti (144), though not actually essential to the history of modern sculpture, were nevertheless prophetic. The return to primordial origins, the *nostalgie de la boue* which Baudelaire describes, are already marked here. Not only the rejection of anthropomorphic proportions is implicit in this work but also the desire to submerge oneself in primitive emotional states. The descriptive aspects of traditional European sculpture disappear and the evocative awe-inspiring qualities of the startlingly unfamiliar form are substituted. Formally, a new freedom is attained in these works. Form is no longer continuous and the relationship between mass and the void in which it expands is no longer attuned to our normal observation of displacement in accordance to principles first described by Archimedes. The later infatuation with Oceanic and African art on the part of the Expressionists and the Cubists is already foreshadowed here. A whole new aesthetic logic in which the standard of beauty is no longer dependent on resemblance to objects outside the work of art but on a satisfying relationship of forms within the limits which the sculpture sets itself is forecast in these remarkable carvings. Also important is the heavy accentuation of the material essence of the sculpture. The graininess of the wood becomes an integral part of the impression made by the sculpture, as is the whittled aspect of all planes which is evidence of the rough gouges that are used.

Cubism, the most important milestone in the history of modern painting, also marked the birth of radically contemporary sculpture. However, it would be a dangerous simplification to equate Cubist painting and Cubist sculpture. Intellectual and speculative in mood, Cubism finds its fullest expression in painting, which, being disembodied to begin with, can more easily reflect and absorb the intricacies of perceptions as complex as those of Cubism. Cubism is concerned, as is pure geometry, not with the substance and the appearance of things but with their inherent qualities. The simultaneous perception of the inside and outside of objects, the analysis of forms in motion and of forms interpenetrating with other forms, the swift dislocation of the point of view from one unstable position to another, equally unstable position, the interchangeability of volume and void . . . these are all aspects of Cubism which can lend themselves to pictorial representation. Sculpture, maintaining its mass and density, even when activated, as happens in the work of Calder, can absorb these principles only to a limited extent.

V Constantin Brancusi
Fish 1930
New York, Museum of Modern
Acquired through
the Lillie P. Bliss Bequest

VI Alexander Calder
Red petals 1942
Chicago, the Arts Club

VII Marcel Duchamp
The large glass (The bride stripped bare by her bachelors, even) 1915–25
Philadelphia Museum of Art
Louise and Walter Arensberg
Collection
(VI & VII *overleaf*)

40

But the suggestions of Cubism were fruitful nevertheless. First of all, the idea of analyzing mass in accordance to its underlying structure and then recomposing this mass with a crystalline interlocking of forms in order to make visible the most powerful interaction between the various forces contained in the structure of a given configuration gave rise to a completely new attitude towards sculpture. In the work of Picasso and Lipchitz, Archipenko and Zadkine (218, 227, 233, 237), the analysis of form and the exposure of the core of their sculptural masses produced sensational results. Sculpture was no longer a mass bounded by an external epidermis. The skin was broken to allow the counteracting forces to be seen which lie behind the surface of things. The surroundings of a figure impinged on the figure itself and space began to flood into sculptural form in the same ratio in which sculptural form reached outward in order to take possession of surrounding space.

Especially in the work of Lipchitz's early period, the energy of the artist becomes directly visible. The massive hewing process makes itself felt and the spaces between forms appear not only in the guise of voids but, because of their sharply described shapes, evoke the masses which have been cut away and discarded.

Cubism, too, is at the root of Boccioni's and Balla's Futurist sculptures (221, 225). Here, again, the anarchy preached by Boccioni in his manifestoes and speeches found expression more readily in paintings. The magic of motion which transforms the appearance of all things and which is also symbolic of a culture at war with its own traditions, inflamed the imaginations of this important group of artists. Boccioni, the leader of the group, is perhaps the most important exponent of Cubist theory. His sculptures like *Bottle in Space* (222) are more readily understandable than the more hermetic work of Picasso and Lipchitz. Yet in his most important work, *Continuity in Space* (221), he kept alive one of the most important fundamentals of Italian art: its essentially communicative nature and its admiration of the human shape. The figure, despite its machine-manufactured look, shows that the artist has a certain Classical love for fluent, expansive motion. Balla, on the other hand, came to quite different conclusions in his totally abstract sculptures. Some of them, constructed of wire in order to give utmost preponderance to the corroding force of space and time, finally liberated future sculptors from all obligations to recognizable forms. Partially inspired by the Futurists' breakthrough to pure sculptural abstraction, and encouraged by the boldness of Russian revolutionary tendencies, latent in the years before 1916, overt thereafter, the Constructivists strove towards a new formal beauty which

III Richard Lippold
Variations within a sphere No. 10.
The sun 1953–6
New York, Metropolitan
Museum of Art
Fletcher Fund 1956
Base: l/h edge

would have all the clarity of a geometric proposition combined with the structural firmness of an ideal architectural concept. The blending and inter-penetration of sculptural and architectural functions comes out most strongly in Tatlin's destroyed work. It would be hard to class this enigmatic and immensely talented artist among the architects or the sculptors of this period. But even in the more unequivocally sculptural works of Gabo and Pevsner, there is always the feeling of the blueprint, i.e. of the most pared down disembodied representation of a structural idea. This purity of expression is paralleled by the work of the independent but similarly inclined artists who are loosely grouped with the de Stijl movement, especially Vantongerloo (250, 252). Today, this tendency remains strongly operative in the work of such very different artists as Bill and Lippold (255, 256, 305, VIII).

The secularization of forms which had been operative since Neoclassicism finally comes to its logical conclusion in the work of Marcel Duchamp. If there is no spiritual hierarchy of values, one form is as valid as another. We come to the total democratization of form which Duchamp sardonically presents to us in his ready-mades. In a world which admires both the machine on the one hand and totally disembodied speculation on the other, *Bottlerack* (258) fulfils many functions and answers many desires . . . as well as posing a whole new realm of important questions. Physically, *Bottlerack* responds to our admiration for the anonymously manufactured article, spiritually it appeals to our adulation of the physics formula. Taken as an abstract form, it can be analyzed in traditional terms of balance, space-mass relationship, harmony of corresponding forms, etc. Taken as a concrete presence, *Bottle-rack*, wrenched from its daily, practical use, is fascinating by being more completely itself than any work of art, having behind it all the accidents of the artist's birth, talent and training, ever could be. This horned object on a pedestal is a completely expressive idol of our century and Duchamp fulfils, in this instance, the ancient prerogative of all sculptors: he is the magician who discovers the enigma of an obscure world which underlies appearances, erupting at moments to confound us. His pioneering action remains impor-tant even in our own day in the work of what is called Neo-Dada or Pop Art (260, 344).

Duchamp spans the gap which lies between the ruthlessly objective, speculative world of Cubism, a world which he at once celebrates and contradicts, and the opposed world of Surrealism which attaches subjective importance to even the most trivial or accidental act. Where the Cubist investigated such phenomena as mass, space, time, motion, appearance and structure for their own sake, the Surrealist sees in every action and in every visible or invisible object a profound and disturbing meaning. Trance, dream, ecstasy, these are the states in which we can perceive relationships and intuitive significance in the otherwise menacing, disparate clutter of the world. Beyond the accidental coming together of irrelevant objects we begin to perceive that it is our will, or our yearning, which have worked in dark, subconscious ways to bring about these accidents. Here, again, the programme of Surrealist thought is easier to express in painting than it is in sculpture. The evanescence of the dream, the moodiness of buried desires defy representation in dense and solid forms with which we are confronted in sculpture. Yet, by detaching themselves from the more dogmatic core of Surrealist artists, two artists in particular have achieved greatness. Jean Arp's organic shapes always threaten to dissolve . . . like the clouds which were consulted by ancient augurs. They are hauntingly reminiscent of some elusive experience which we may have had or dreamed about, and they also introduce us to a world of growing, expanding and contracting forms in which the very essence of the life process, continuous metamorphosis, seems to be captured (268–71). Lipchitz, too, became involved in the new world of the subconscious opened up by Surrealism. The implacable stare of some of his figures and fluid expression of his latest semi-automatic sculptures (290) where the subconscious rises to the surface, lead us into realms of experience which had never before manifested themselves in so pure a form. Some of these sculptures have been erroneously likened to the famous Rorschach test in which the subject 'sees' certain associative forms in an amorphous, irregular blot. It is true that the dictates of the subconscious are strong in Lipchitz's automatic sculptures. But whereas the Rorschach test represents the projection of the subject's subconscious on to a deliberately impersonal, essentially blank screen (the blot) which he then goes on to interpret in the light of his own fears and desires, Lipchitz's procedure starts with the fear, the anxiety or the faceless desire of the artist which is allowed to manifest itself by shaping forms which will be expressive of these inward states.

Lipchitz, who has participated – but always at a great distance – in all the major movements of this century, is the most symbolic figure in the history of modern sculpture. He is always willing to learn but he is never willing to give up his personal intuition and integrity by joining a trend. In this way, some of the major contemporary sculptors cannot be fitted into any pre-established category.

This is certainly the case with Brancusi. Considering that he is generally admitted to be the greatest sculptor of our century, relatively little has been written about him, and his work has escaped critical manipulations as well as constricting affiliations with various movements. There is little that is polemical in his work, and he seldom falls back on extra-artistic sustenance in the way that the Surrealists fall back on depth-psychology. His art is not an aggressive one and, in an age which demands powerful stimulants, his success is due more to the endurance of the new sculptural vocabulary he engendered than to its shock quality. Brancusi does not challenge confrontation, nor does he call out to his public. Yet not even the staunchest defender of the dullest Academic traditions can remain unaware of the immense potency of his work.

Brancusi is concerned with the universal powers of death, rebirth, fertility and fallowness and, consequently, most of his sculptures fulfil the functions of both flower and seed. They are at once the full expression, the ripest stage of a living cycle of continual metamorphosis and they are also the starkly concentrated, promising but unpretentious seed (186–94). Whether one approaches them as naïve, simple objects – the toys of a genius – or whether one meditates on them as complex expressions of the most sophisticated knowledge which sums up Oriental as well as Western experience, one is invariably welcomed by Brancusi: the innocent and the astutely wise are equally satisfied by him.

Brancusi's work contains, overtly or implicitly, almost all the most important theories of art which were to follow in his wake. The 'ready-made' and the *objet-trouvé* are apparent in his simplified forms, which, in their extreme polish and streamlining, have all the marks of belonging to an age dominated by the machine – it dominates all but Brancusi. At the same time, he is religiously attentive to minute variations, asymmetries and individualizations which testify to the prodigious variety of nature. His stones remain fully and coherently stones. Yet the imprint of the master's hand is always in evidence (187).

A noble anonymity, a willingness to let his sculptures live independent lives, is eloquent in all of his works. Superficially this tendency resembles the anonymity of Duchamp who, by hiding behind objects which he has chosen but not made, disappears from the scene. But whereas Duchamp's anonymity is ironic or even satanic, Brancusi's is more like that of a priest who, pointing away from himself towards the mysteries he celebrates, effaces himself in humility.

Like Brancusi, two of the most influential and qualitatively exalted sculptors, Gonzalez and Calder, defy identification with movements. Gonzalez's work opened up a totally new welding technique which in itself is expressive of our century. This process, utterly unlike the traditional means of carving or moulding, puts individual elements in juxtaposition with each other, permits radically new ponderations as well as a new sense of gesture based on the dialogue between disparate and self-assertive elements. Again the declaration of the physical nature of his tools and material (welding-torch and sheet-metal) are insisted on. Yet Gonzalez, and in this he is only rivalled by Brancusi, infuses an ardent, very human monumentality into his sculptures. His master-work, *Montserrat* (313), is one of the few sculptures of our times which can be said to have changed human vision and perception. Piercing isolated experience, Gonzalez discovered a full expression of the modern condition just as Michelangelo and Bernini had managed, in their sculptures, to go from their own limited experience and understanding of their epoch to a statement which fully incorporates an intelligible *summa* of the basic relationship between man and his era.

Calder, too, eludes classification. Several artists before him added mobility to their sculpture either by hidden motors or by suspension in mid-air. Yet only he managed to integrate motion with mass in such a way that the final result was not a freakish experiment but a viable, if fanciful, artistic expression. His mobiles are never tricky. They are the outgrowth of an intimate and very poetic sympathy with everything which grows in accordance with a logical but inimitable pattern. Certainly Cubism and maybe even Futurism and Surrealism form a backdrop to Calder's epochal sculptures. But his art maintains itself at an equidistant point between all programmatic tendencies.

Our understanding of modern sculpture would be extremely limited if it did not include a thorough acquaintance with those artists who eschew the experimental by keeping to more traditional values in their sculptures without, however, leaving the demands of our era unanswered. Maillol and Bourdelle are perhaps the foremost artists of this group. These artists, each in a pronouncedly personal way, rescue for us an important heritage which had been traduced and dispersed by their Academic, imitative ancestors. Maillol's art is all subtlety: a serene and overjoyed rediscovery of harmonies pertaining to the human body. A slight shift in proportion, a nuance in the stance is all that ever differentiates his sculptures from each other or from their Classical forebears. Yet this slight shift and varied nuance are all that is necessary to give unquestionably modern life to his forms. Bourdelle, whose fame is just about to be reborn among artists and connoisseurs of the younger generation, is more haunted than Maillol. He does not revive the primordial Mediterranean sense of equilibrated power as does Maillol. There is also alive in him the other half of the French tradition, the force that is responsible for the enigmatic pathos of French medieval sculpture. The impotence of man, an intuitive understanding of the destruction which must come to all things, is always latent in his work, though not in that of Maillol. Both artists, however, share an immense respect for impeccable execution. Technique and finish are uplifted by them to a region in which these essentially craftsmanlike attributes become symbolic of the artist's faith in the earnestness of what he is doing.

★   ★   ★

The post-war scene is as bewildering as it is exhilarating. Even geographically there is no fixed centre of gravity. Not Paris but a multitude of centres must be watched carefully if one is to garner an adequate picture of today's sculptural efforts. Tokyo, New York, South America, Denmark . . . one can put one's finger practically anywhere on the map and land in a place where worth-while and possibly even great sculptural activity is under way.

But, be it due to clever publicity, to the timely appearance of an art which fulfils a widespread public need, or to sheer talent, the mind turns involuntarily to Neo-Dada and Pop Art whenever the question of *avant-garde* sculpture arises today. The artists who are loosely connected with this blanket title, Johns, Rauschenberg, Segal, Tinguely, Chamberlain, display one trait in common: they present, under a hundred different guises, sometimes earnestly, sometimes jovially and sometimes ironically, objects which have been suddenly severed from their ordinary environment and plunged instead into the realm of aesthetic speculation or simply of sensuous experience. They all seem obsessed with the very understandable notion that our modern condition, shaped by revolutionary scientific, psychological, sociological and political discoveries, has made imperative a new appraisal of our no-longer familiar habitat. In this respect, these artists as well as their colleagues whose work is generally classed as 'assemblage' are indebted to Duchamp. The disquieting undercurrents which are evoked in us by much of this work also recall Surrealism.

The muscular enthusiasm of these artists, their high intelligence and convincing humour give them a very individual stamp and save them from eclecticism. Their submission to the caprices of chance and their exaltation of 'gesture', that is to say, the direct communication of the ardour, the energy and the chronological sequence with which the artist develops his image: the presentation of the climactic moment of choice in which the artist feels himself compelled to follow one out of many suggestions which the incomplete work throws out to him in challenge make an association of these artists with Abstract Expressionism possible. However, Pop Art and Neo-Dada and Neo-Realism are all at least in partial rebellion against their Abstract-Expressionist ancestors.

46

Jackson Pollock, de Kooning and Motherwell are essentially aristocrats in their attitude towards their vocation. If they feel free and utterly independent of the laws which bind ordinary mortals, they also are loyal to the spirit of *noblesse oblige*: they may seem aloof and even indecipherable, but their good faith can never be questioned. They follow the dictates of their destinies.

Pop Artists, by virtue of their freedom from convention and by virtue of their authoritative, sometimes insolent appearance are also aristocrats . . . but they are aristocrats out slumming. The Abstract Expressionist rouses us to ask important questions concerning the dignity of the artist, concerning the possibility of a new beauty in our world, concerning the emotional and sensuous revelations which art can bring to us. The Pop Artist bemuses. The artist of the Abstract Expressionist movement puts his work into a complementary relationship with the familiar but unfathomable world in which we live. He takes full responsibility for its creation. He points to the infinite gap which exists between true art and sham mass-produced culture. His work, in the last analysis, depends on quality. The Pop Artist, rather than take responsibility for what he creates, prefers to present us with intelligently chosen fragments, which, regarded in relationship to the artist's abstruse construction of such fragments, suddenly take on a new and unexpected meaning . . . often, they even take on an unexpected beauty. What interests him in this process is the curious situation which is set up: in a world in which the sham has become a norm in its own right, a work of art which is a composite of shams will necessarily be a more revealing, a 'truer' work of art in exact ratio to its spuriousness. The artist abdicates all his prerogatives except that of choice. His work pretends to be an ordinary, mass-produced item (or the simulacrum of such an article), just as the aristocrats of the later eighteenth century, taking their Rousseau seriously, pretended to be shepherds and milk-maids. As long as the 'pretend' element is strongly visible, as long as the artist can juggle both the artificial and the real elements of his work, showing us that he is still at the controls even though he *seems* to have relaxed all hold over his materials, as long as he can do this, he is safe. The danger lies in his reaching a point at which the pretended and the actual become perfectly congruent and are no longer separable. Just as the eighteenth-century aristocrat found himself in danger when no one could recognize him for what he was and, taking him at his word, judged him as shepherd or milk-maid and found him to be impractical, useless and, worst of all, no longer amusing.

In general, the search for stable realities, which first became urgent when the fixed centre of the universe began to be questioned under the impact of secularization, continues taking on the most varied formulations, and with constantly increasing tempo as time seems to run out for civilization such as we know it. Especially for the sculptor, dealing as he does in corporeal substance, it is essential that even the lowliest objects should contain their own degree of significance, that they have a place in the world and are not merely irrelevant clutter. It is no accident that Rilke, still the most profound interpreter of Rodin, begins his book* on Rodin's sculptures by a discussion of things as such, the magic of their appearance, their puzzling aggressiveness, the capacity for satisfying or irritating. In many ways we have come full circle and have actually arrived back at the primordial origins of sculpture when man first discovered that a lonely boulder or a gnarled tree, by being utterly dissociated from their next of kin, had the power to inspire awe and lead the mind to dwell on eternally inscrutable forces.

1 Jean-Antoine Houdon
S. Bruno 1766
Rome, Sta Maria degli Ang(

* Rainer Maria Rilke, *Rodin*, Fischer Bücherei, Frankfurt/Hamburg, 1956.

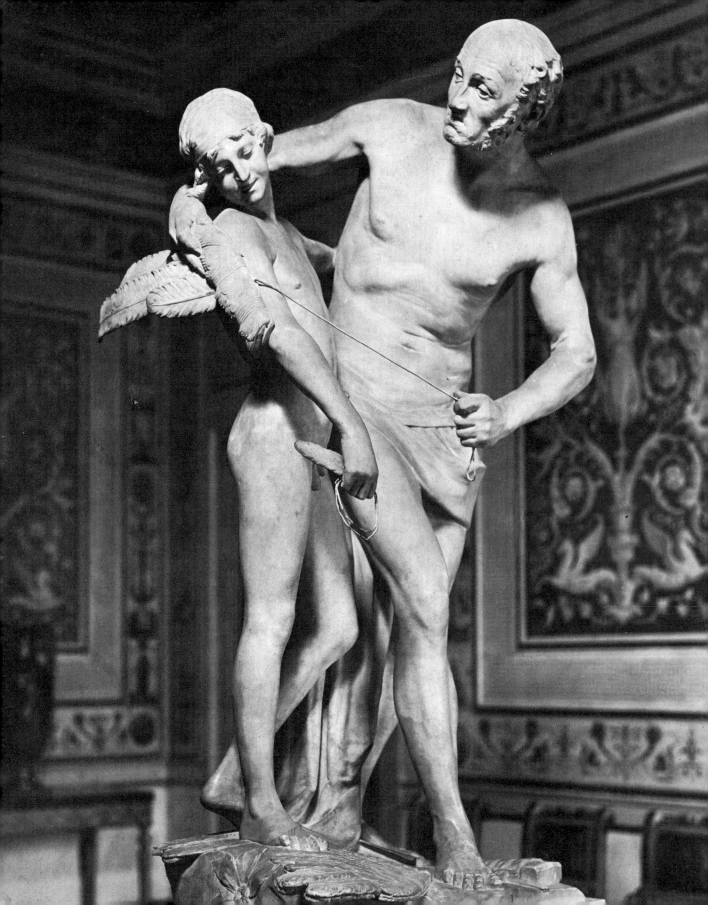

Antonio Canova
Daedalus and Icarus 1779
Venice, Museo Correr

Antonio Canova
Briseis surrendered to the heralds of Agamemnon 1790
Possagno, Gipsoteca Canoviana

Antonio Canova
Cupid and Psyche 1793
New York, Metropolitan
Museum of Art
Gift of Isador Strauss, 1905

5 Antonio Canova
Tomb of Clement XIV 1784–7
Rome, SS. Apostoli

6 Antonio Canova
Monument to Angelo Emo 1792–5
Venice, Museo Storico Navale

ANGELO EMO

7 Antonio Canova
Hebe 1816
Forlì, Pinacoteca

8 Antonio Canova
Hercules and Lycas 1812–15
Rome, Galleria Nazionale
d'Arte Moderna

CLEMENTI·XIII·
REZZONICO·
P·M·
FRATRIS·FILII·

9 Antonio Canova
Tomb of Pope Clement XIII
1787–92
Rome, St Peter's

10 Antonio Canova
Tomb of Archduchess Maria Christina
1798–1805
Vienna, Augustinerkirche

1 Antonio Canova
Napoleon 1803–11
Milan, Palazzo di Brera

2 Antonio Canova
Paolina Bonaparte Borghese 1805–8
Rome, Galleria Borghese

13 Bertel Thorvaldsen
Ganymede with Jupiter as the eagle 1817
Copenhagen, Thorvaldsens Museum

15 Bertel Thorvaldsen
Jason with the Golden Fleece 1802–3
Copenhagen, Thorvaldsens Museum

Bertel Thorvaldsen
Angel holding a font 1839
Copenhagen, Church of Our Lady

Bertel Thorvaldsen
Annunciation 1842
Copenhagen, Thorvaldsens Museum

18 Gaetano Monti
The Allied Sovereigns arrive at Leipzig 1826
Milan, Arco della Pace (*foot of page*)

21 John Flaxman
Monument to Lord Mansfield 1795–1801
London, Westminster Abbey

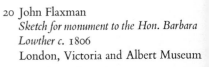

20 John Flaxman
Sketch for monument to the Hon. Barbara Lowther c. 1806
London, Victoria and Albert Museum

19 Johan Heinrich von Dannecker
Ariadne on a panther 1803
Stuttgart, Staatsgalerie

SACRED TO THE MEMORY OF HARRIET SUSAN, VISCOUNTESS FITZHARRIS,
GHTER OF FRANCIS BATEMAN DASHWOOD ESQ! OF WELL VALE, IN THE COUNTY OF LINCOLN,
D-WIFE OF JAMES EDWARD VISCOUNT FITZHARRIS, OF HERON COURT IN THIS PARISH,
WHERE SHE DEPARTED THIS LIFE ON MONDAY NIGHT SEPTEMBER THE 4, 1815,
IN THE 32! YEAR OF HER AGE.

FLAXMAN,
R.A.
SCULPTOR.

22 John Flaxman
*Monument to Harriet Susan,
Viscountess Fitzharris c.* 1815
Hampshire, Christchurch Priory

23 Sir Francis Chantrey
Mrs Jordan as Charity 1831–4
Bletchingley, Surrey
Earl of Munster Collection

Matthew Cotes Wyatt
Monument to Princess Charlotte 1820–4
Windsor, St George's Chapel

Pierre Giraud
Sketch for his wife's tomb 1827
Paris, Louvre

Sir Richard Westmacott
Monument to Charles James Fox
1810–23
London, Westminster Abbey

CHARLES JAMES FOX
B: 24. JAN. 1749. N:S:
D: 13. SEPT: 1806

Joseph-Charles Marin
Arcadian family c. 1790
New York, French & Company, Inc.

28 Joseph-Charles Marin
Caius Gracchus leaving his wife,
Licinia 1801
Paris, École des Beaux-Arts

29 Simon-Louis Boizot
Apollon Musagète c. 1786
Sèvres, Musée Céramique

30 Antoine-Denis Chaudet
Amor catching a butterfly
Completed posthumously (model 1802
Paris, Louvre

31 Joseph Chinard
Madame Récamier c. 1802
Lyon, Musée des Beaux-Arts

32 Antonio Canova
Madame Récamier 1813
Possagno, Gipsoteca Canoviana

3 Joseph Chinard
Apollo crushing Superstition underfoot
1791
Paris, Musée Carnavalet

34 Gottfried Schadow
   Monument to Princess Louise and Prir
   Friederike of Mecklenburg-Schwerin 1
   Berlin, Staatliche Museen

35 Gottfried Schadow
   Tomb of Graf Alexander von der Ma
   1787–91
   Berlin, Dorotheenstädtische Kirche

Christian-Daniel Rauch
Tomb of Queen Louise c. 1815
Berlin, Charlottenburg Mausoleum

Asmus-Jakob Carstens
One of the Fates 1794
Frankfurt a.M., Städelsches Kunstinstitut

38 Johan Tobias Sergel
Mars and Venus 1771-2
Gothenburg, Konstmuseum

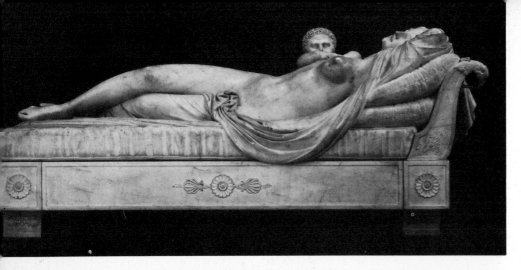

39 Johan-Niklas Byström
Juno and the infant Hercules c. 1828
Stockholm, Nationalmuseum

40 John Gibson
Hylas and the water-nymphs 1826
London, Tate Gallery

41 Hiram Powers
The Greek slave 1846
Washington, D.C., Corcoran
Gallery of Art

42 William Rush
Comedy and Tragedy 1808
Philadelphia, Pa, Pennsylvania
Academy of the Fine Arts

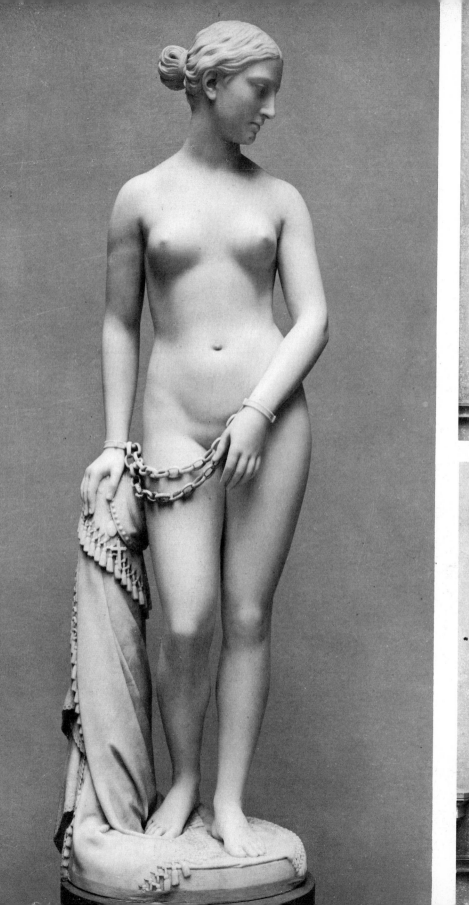

43 Valentin Sonnenschein
Portrait of a Berne alderman c. 1780
Berne, Kunstmuseum

44 Bartolomeo Pinelli
The wounded brigand c. 1830
Rome, Museo di Roma

45 & 46 Lorenzo Bartolini
Trust in God 1835
Milan, Museo Poldi-Pezzoli

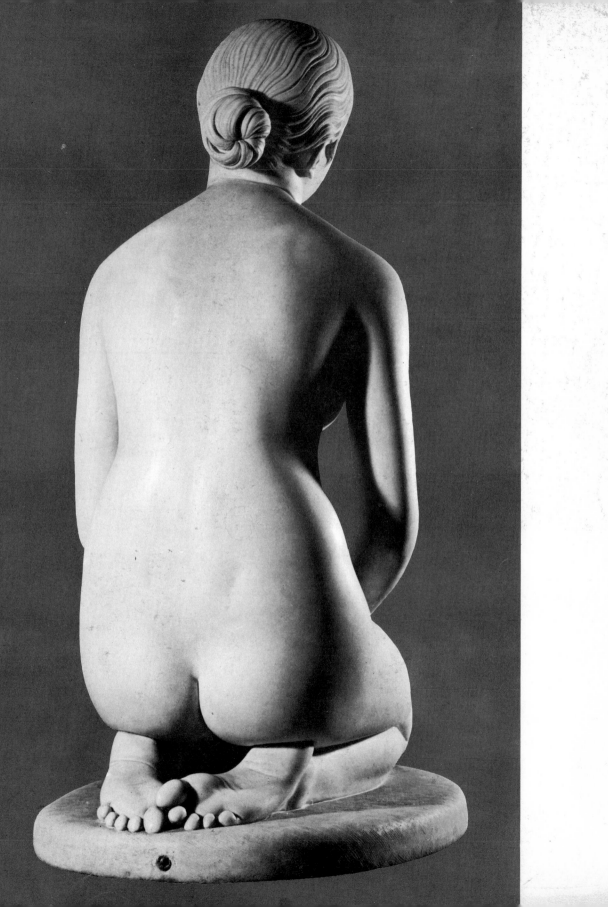

47 Lorenzo Bartolini
The wine-presser c. 1842–4
Florence, Marchese Bufalini Collection

48 & 49 Lorenzo Bartolini
Monument to Princess
Czartoryski of Warsaw 1837–44
Florence, Sta Croce

50 Jean-Pierre Cortot
*Marie-Antoinette
succoured by religion c.* 1827
Paris, Chapelle Expiatoire

51 François-Joseph Bosio
Apotheosis of Louis XVI 1825
Paris, Chapelle Expiatoire

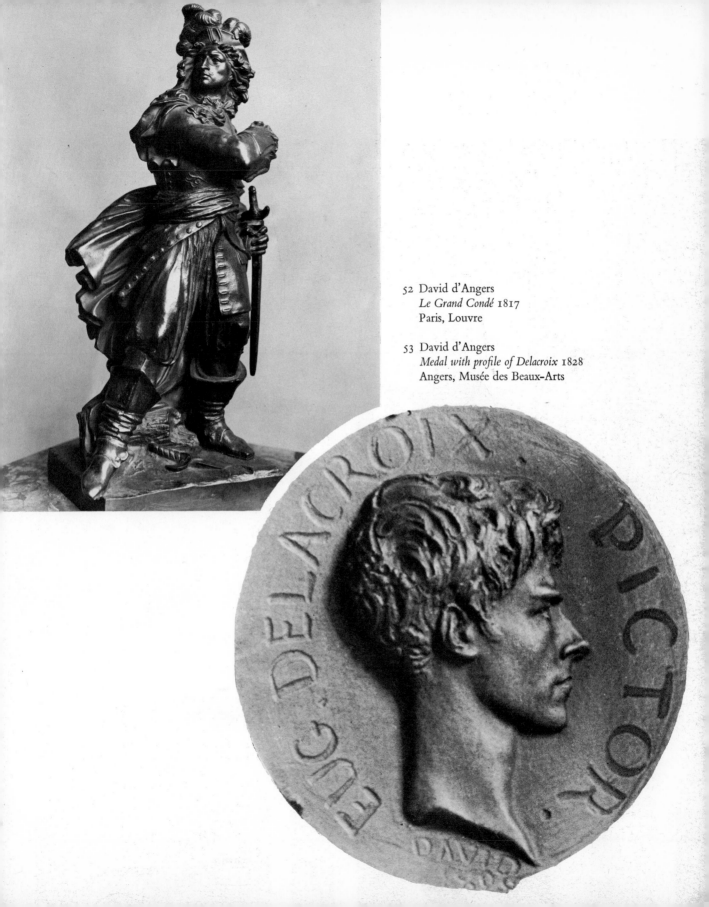

52 David d'Angers
Le Grand Condé 1817
Paris, Louvre

53 David d'Angers
Medal with profile of Delacroix 1828
Angers, Musée des Beaux-Arts

David d'Angers
Nicolò Paganini 1830
Angers, Musée des Beaux-Arts

David d'Angers
Battle of Fleuris. General Jourdan
refuses to accept his enemy's sword 1835
Angers, Musée des Beaux-Arts

David d'Angers
Pediment of the Panthéon 1837
Angers, Musée des Beaux-Arts

57 François Rude
Mercury 1834
Paris, Louvre

58 François Rude
Neapolitan fisherboy with tortoise 18
Paris, Louvre

59 François Rude
Marshal Ney 1852–3
Paris, Avenue de l'Observatoire

60 François Rude
La Marseillaise 1833–6
Paris, Arc de Triomphe

61 François Rude
Tomb of
Godefroi de Cavaignac 1845–7
Paris, Cimetière de Montmartre

62 François Rude
Napoleon awakening to immortality 1845
Paris, Louvre

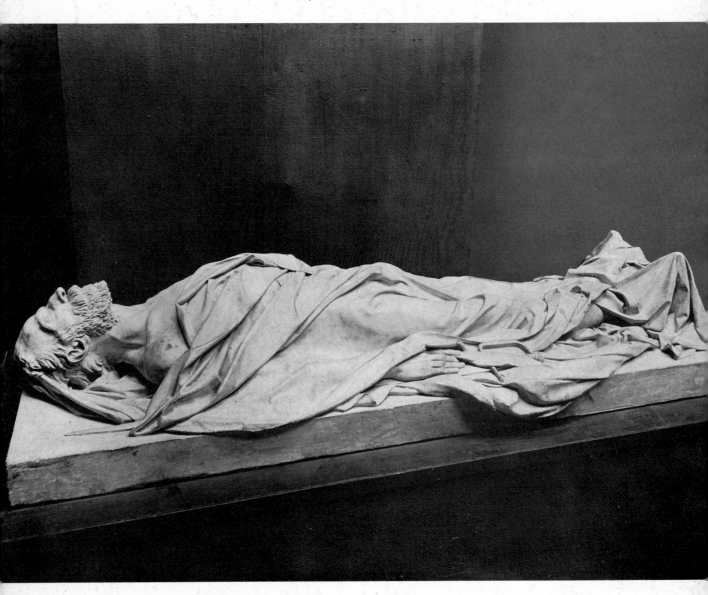

& 64 Antoine-Augustin Préault
Christ on the Cross 1840
Paris, Église St Gervais-et-St Protais

Antoine-Augustin Préault
Massacre 1834
Chartres, Musée des Beaux-Arts

66 Félicie de Fauveau
Tomb of the sculptress's mother 1858
Florence, Sta Croce

67 Antoine-Augustin Préault
Ophelia 1876 (original 1843)
Marseille, Musée de Longchamps

8 Alexander Munro
Paolo and Francesca 1852
Birmingham, City Museum and
Art Gallery

9 Théodore Géricault
Nymph and satyr 1817–20
Buffalo, N.Y., Albright–Knox Gallery
George B. and Jenny R. Matthews Fund

70 Antoine-Louis Barye
   Theseus and the Minotaur 1849–52
   Paris, Louvre

71 Antoine-Louis Barye
   Fortitude protecting Labour 1859
   Paris, Louvre

72 Antoine-Louis Barye
Bull attacked by a tiger
Exhibited posthumously
Paris, Louvre

73 Antoine-Louis Barye
Jaguar devouring a hare 1852
Paris, Louvre (*see* 182)

74 Antoine-Louis Barye
Napoleon on horseback 1856
Paris, Louvre

5 Antoine-Louis Barye
Young nude woman 1846
Paris, Louvre

6 Jean-Jacques Pradier
Laundress c. 1850
Geneva, Musée d'Art et d'Histoire

7 Jean-Baptiste Clésinger
Woman bitten by a serpent 1847
Paris, Louvre

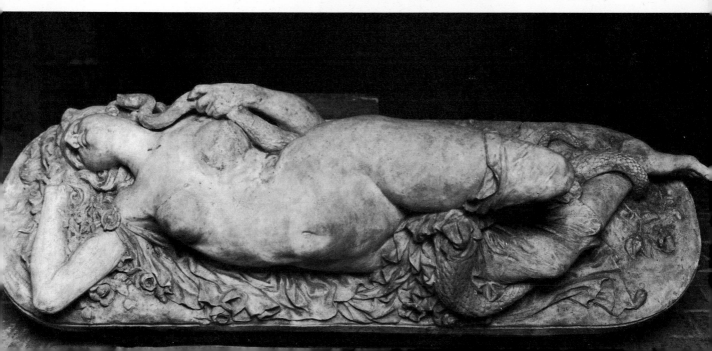

78 Honoré Daumier
The burden c. 1855
Paris, Paul Rosenberg Collection

79 Jean-Pierre Dantan
   Balzac 1835
   Paris, Musée Carnavalet

80 Honoré Daumier
   Migrants c. 1870
   Paris, Geoffrey-Déchaume Collection

Honoré Daumier
The orator c. 1832
Marseille, Musée des Beaux-Arts

Honoré Daumier
Toothless laughter c. 1832
Marseille, Musée des Beaux-Arts

Honoré Daumier
Prunelle c. 1830–2
Marseille, Musée des Beaux-Arts

84 Honoré Daumier
Self-portrait c. 1855
Paris, Bibliothèque Nationale

85 Honoré Daumier
Ratapoil 1850
Paris, Louvre

86 Francisque-Joseph Duret
St Michael overcoming the Devil 1860–1
Paris, Place Saint-Michel

Jean-Baptiste Carpeaux
Ugolino and his children 1860–2
Valenciennes, Musée des Beaux-Arts

Jean-Baptiste Carpeaux
Bruno Chérier 1875
Paris, Louvre

Jean-Baptiste Carpeaux
Mademoiselle Fiocre 1869
Paris, Louvre

90 Jean-Baptiste Carpeaux
Flora 1866
Paris, Louvre

91 Jean-Baptiste Carpeaux
Fontaine de l'Observatoire:
the four quarters of the globe 1868–9
Paris, Jardin du Luxembourg

92 Jean-Baptiste Carpeaux
The dance 1868–9
Paris, façade of the Opéra

93 Adriano Cecioni
Cocotte 1875
Milan, J. Gabriolo Collection

94 Giovanni Dupré
Abel 1842
Florence, Galleria d'Arte Moderna

95 & 96 Achille D'Orsi
Fantasy – Sleep
Fiesole, Villa Dupré

7 Pietro Magni
   *Monument to commemorate the cutting
   of the Suez Canal* 1858–63
   Trieste, Civico Museo Revoltella

8 Albert-Ernest Carrier-Belleuse
   Triton carrying a nymph c. 1860
   London, David Barclay Ltd

Alfred Stevens
Monument to the Duke of
Wellington erected 1875
London, St Paul's Cathedral

o Carlo Marochetti
  Monument to Emanuele Filiberto 1838
  Turin, Piazza San Carlo

4 & 105 Aimé-Jules Dalou
Triomphe de la République 1899
Paris, Place de la Nation

106 Aimé-Jules Dalou
Sketch for the monument to Labour 1889–91
London, Bourdon House

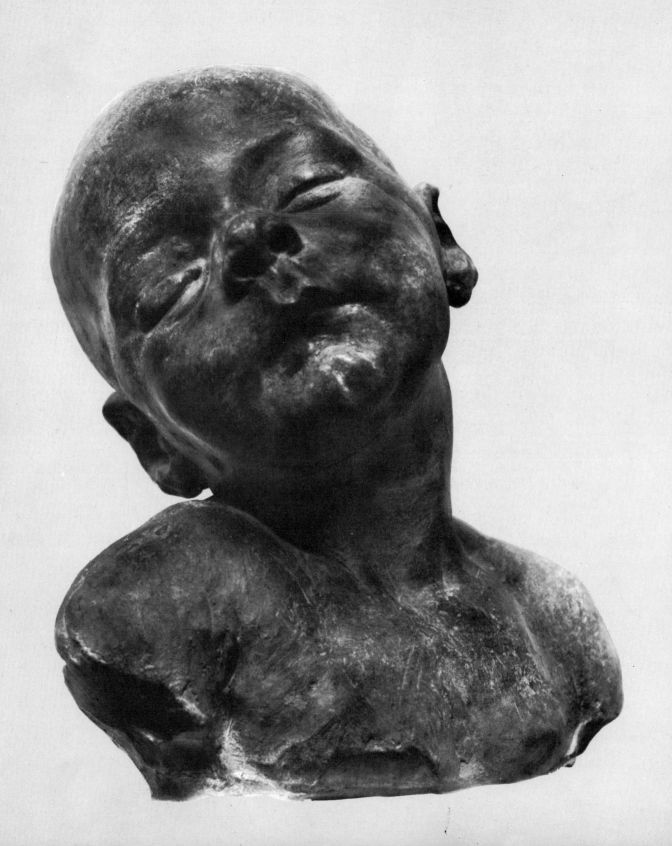

7 Aimé-Jules Dalou
Head of sleeping baby 1878
Paris, Musée du Petit Palais

108 Aimé-Jules Dalou
Woman taking off her stockings c. 1870–80
London, Tate Gallery, gift of Mrs Charles Gordon

109 Designed by M. Panissera,
model by Luigi Belli
Executed by students
of the Royal Academy, Turin
*Monument to the completion
of the Fréjus Tunnel* 1879
Turin, Piazza dello Statuto

110 Constantin Meunier
The stevedore 1903
Antwerp, Suikerrui

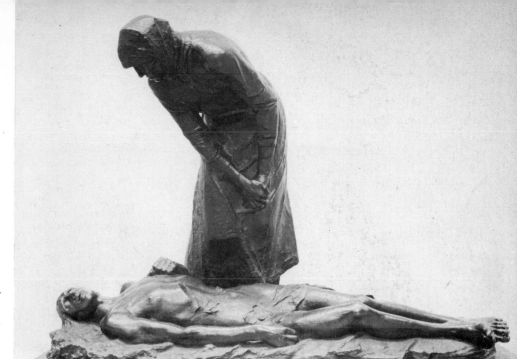

1 Constantin Meunier
   Fire-damp 1903
   Brussels, Musée Constantin Meunier

2 Vincenzo Vela
   Victims of labour
   Ligornetto, Museo Vela

113 Vincenzo Vela
Tomb of Contessa d' Adda 1849
Ligornetto, Museo Vela

114 Auguste Rodin
Mask of man with a broken nose 18
Paris, Musée Rodin

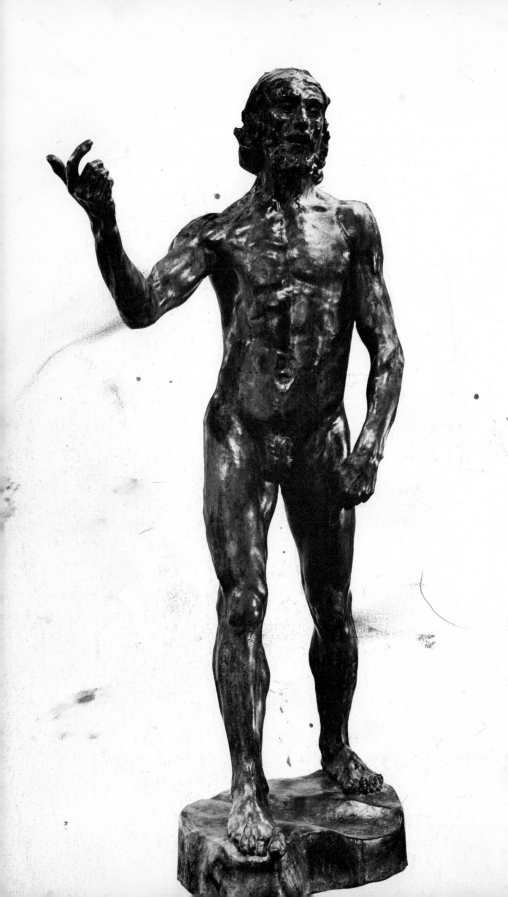

117 Auguste Rodin
St John the Baptist preaching 1878
New York, Museum of Modern Art

118 & 119 Auguste Rodin
The old courtesan
(la belle qui fut la heaulmière) c. 1885
118 New York, Metropolitan Museum
of Art, gift of Thomas F. Ryan, 1910
119 Paris, Musée Rodin

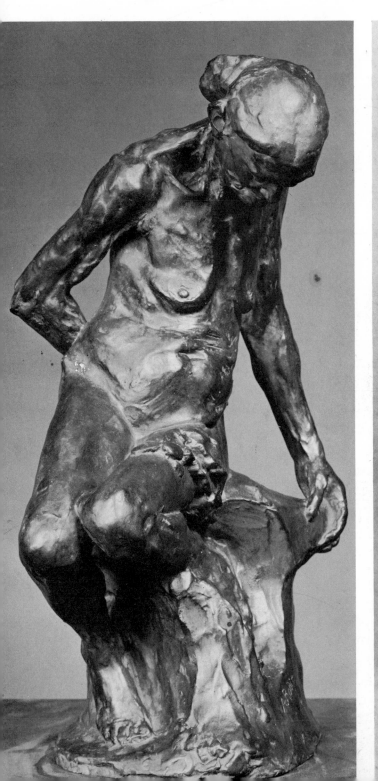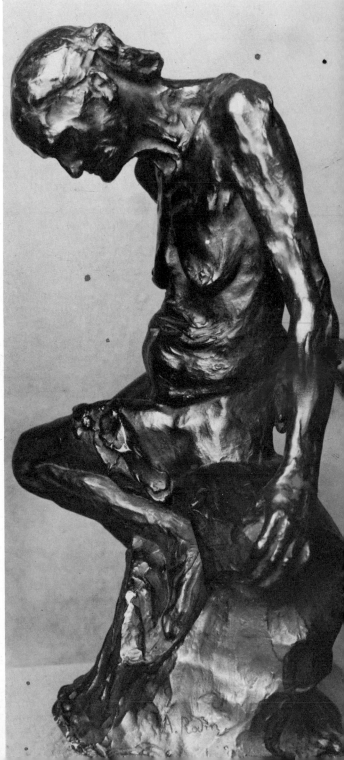

120 Auguste Rodin
The gates of Hell 1880,
exhibited 1900
Rodin Museum, Philadelphia Museum of Art

121 Auguste Rodin
The gates of Hell 1880 (model)
Paris, Musée Rodin

122 Auguste Rodin
The gates of Hell 1880 (detail)
Paris, Musée Rodin

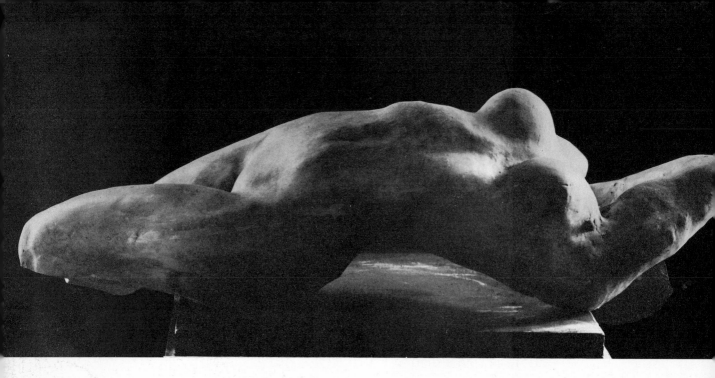

123 Auguste Rodin
Torso of Adèle 1882
Paris, Musée Rodin

124 Auguste Rodin
Iris, messenger of the gods 1890–1
New York, Joseph H. Hirshhorn
Collection

125 Auguste Rodin
The prodigal son c. 1885
Oberlin College, Ohio
Allen Memorial Art Museum
R. J. Miller Fund

126 Auguste Rodin
Le pas de deux c. 1910–13
Paris, Musée Rodin

7, 128 & 129 Auguste Rodin
The burghers of Calais 1885–95
127 & 129 Basle, Kunstmuseum
128 Paris, Musée Rodin

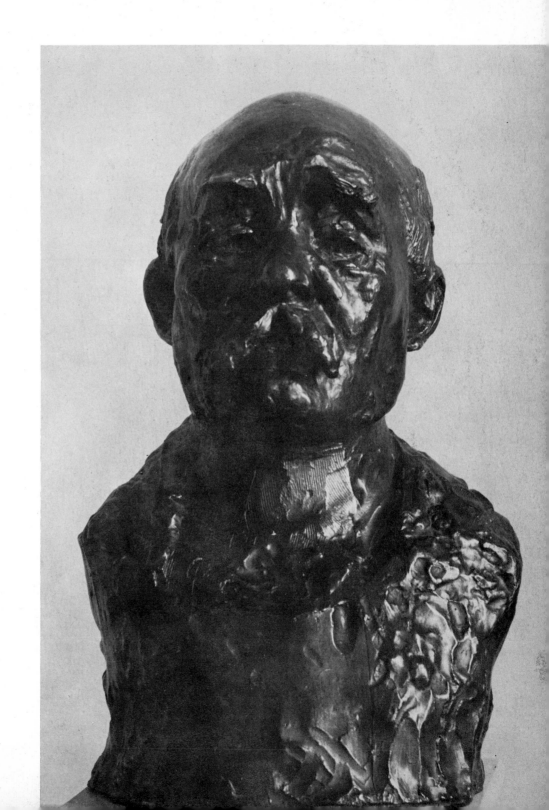

50 Auguste Rodin
Monument to Balzac 1897
New York, Museum
of Modern Art
Presented in memory of
Curt Valentin by his friends

51 Auguste Rodin
Clemenceau 1911
Paris, Musée Rodin

134 Edgar Degas
Arabesque over the right leg c. 1890–5

135 Edgar Degas
The bow c. 1900

136 & 137 Edgar Degas
The little ballet dancer, 14 years old 1880
134–6 New York, Metropolitan Muse
of Art. Bequest of Mrs H. O. Haveme
1929. The H. O. Havemeyer Collectio
137 Paris, Louvre
(*see* IV)

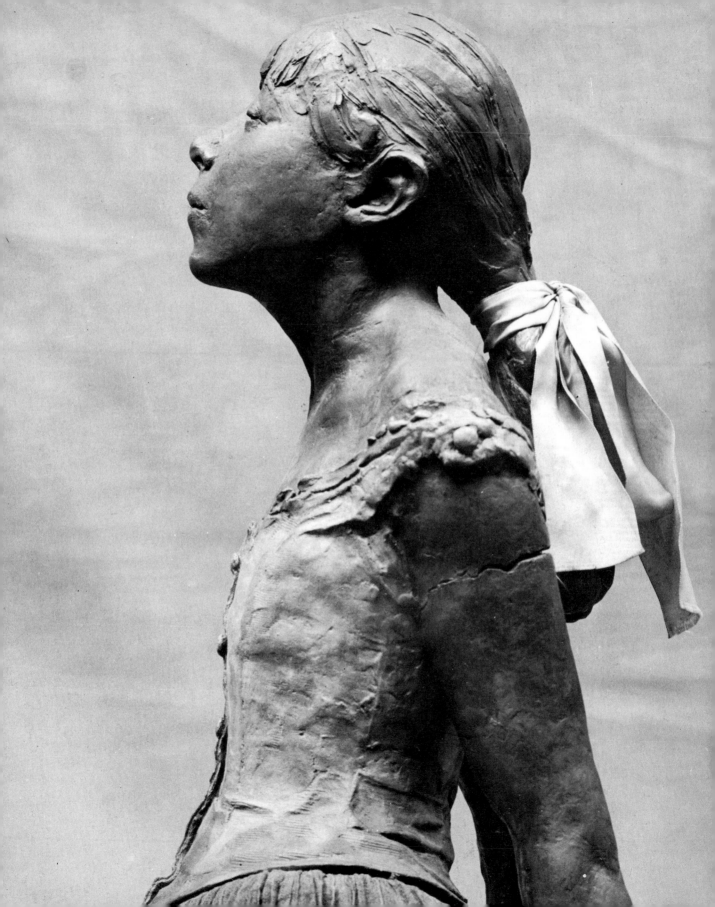

138 Edgar Degas
The tub c. 1886

139 Edgar Degas
The masseuse c. 1896
138–9 New York, Metropolitan
Museum of Art
Bequest of Mrs H. O.
Havemeyer, 1929
The H. O. Havemeyer Collectio

140 Auguste Renoir
The washerwoman 1917
New York, Museum of Modern

141 Auguste Renoir
    The judgement of Paris 1914
    Cleveland Museum of Art
    Purchase from the J. H. Wade Fund

142 César Cros
    Incantation 1892
    Paris, Musée National d'Art Moderne

43 Paul Gauguin
*Soyez amoureuses vous serez
heureuses* 1889–90
Boston, Mass., Museum of Fine Arts

44 Paul Gauguin
Idole (à la coquille) 1900
Paris, private collection

145 Gustave Moreau
Lucretia 1875–80
Paris, Musée Gustave Moreau

146 Giuseppe Grandi
Monument to commemorate the
Five-day Insurrection of 1848
Executed 1894
Milan, Piazzale delle Cinque Giorᵣ

147 Medardo Rosso
Sick boy 1893
New York, Mr and Mrs Samuel
Josefowitz Collection

148 Medardo Rosso
Conversation in a garden 1893
Rome, Galleria Nazionale d'Arte Moderna

149 Medardo Rosso
The bookmaker 1894
New York, Museum of Modern Art
Lillie P. Bliss Bequest

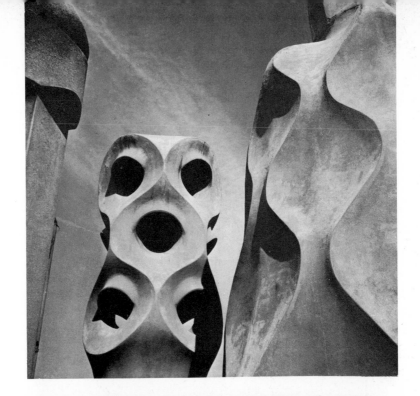

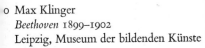

o Max Klinger
Beethoven 1899–1902
Leipzig, Museum der bildenden Künste

,1 Antonio Gaudì
Sculptural chimney-pots 1905–7
Barcelona, Casa Milá

52 Antonio Gaudì
*Figures from the portal of
the Church of the Sagrada Familia* 1884
Barcelona, Calle Provenza

153 Adolf von Hildebrand
Archery lesson 1888
Cologne, Wallraf-Richartz Muse

154 & 155 Adolf von Hildebrand
The Wittelsbach fountain 1844
Munich, Maximilian Platz

156 Ivan Mestrovič
*Caryatids at the tomb
of the Unknown Warrior* 1935–8
Yugoslavia, Mount Avala

157 Paul Bartholomé
Monument to the dead 1899
Paris, Cimetière du Père Lachaise

158 Paul Bartholomé
Tomb of Madame Bartholomé 1887
Bouillant, Crépy-en-Valois

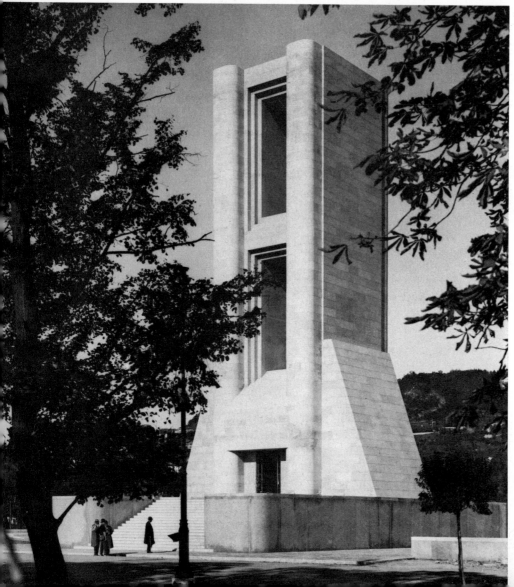

159 Giuseppe Sacconi
Monument to Victor Emmanuel II 1
Rome, Piazza Venezia

160 Adapted from a design for
a lighthouse
made by Antonio Sant'Elia in 19)
Executed by Giuseppe
and Attilio Terragni in 1933
Monument to the fallen
Como

161 Carl Milles
Peace monument 1936
St Paul, Minn., City Hall

162 Gustav Vigeland
Central obelisk c. 1906
Oslo, Frognerpark

63 Paul Manship
Comrades-in-arms 1953
Nettuno, American Cemetery

164 Reg Butler
Unknown political prisoner 1951–2
Berkhamsted, Herts., the artist's collection

165 Aristide Maillol
Mediterranean c. 1901
New York, Museum of Modern Art

66 Aristide Maillol
Desire c. 1904
New York, Museum of Modern Art

167 Aristide Maillol
Pomona 1910
Paris, private collection

168 Aristide Maillol
Spring c. 1910
New York, Metropolitan
Museum of Art
Maynard Fund; from the Museum
of Modern Art, gift of the sculptor

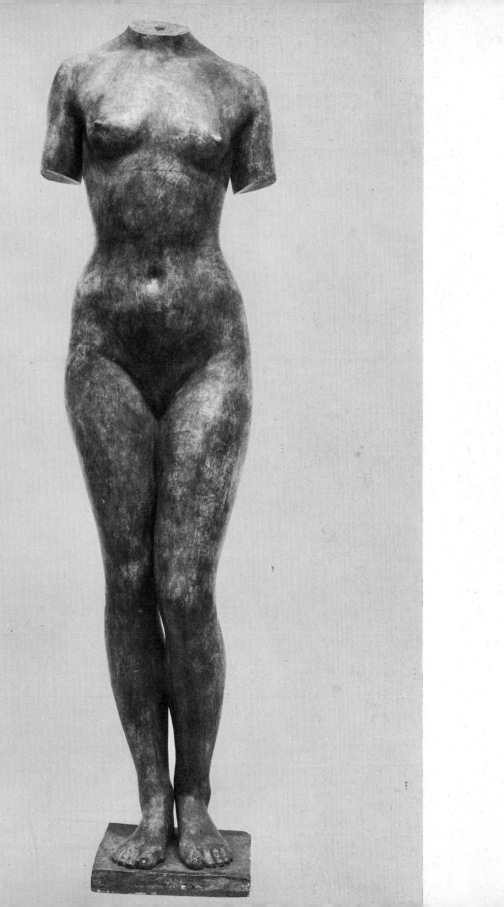

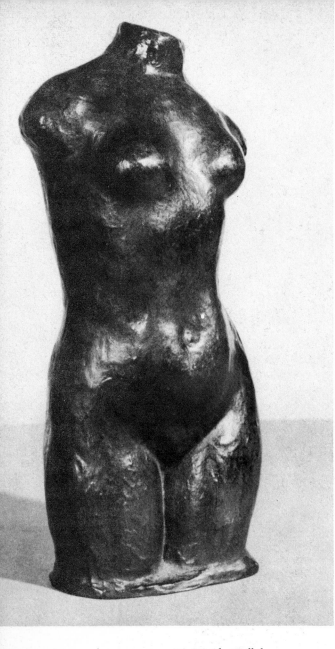

169 Aristide Maillol
Small nude 1910
Paris, Dina Vierny Collection

170 Aristide Maillol
Woman with a necklace 1918–28
London, Tate Gallery

71 Émile-Antoine Bourdelle
St Sebastian 1888
Paris, Musée Bourdelle

2 Émile-Antoine Bourdelle
Hercules the archer 1901
Paris, Musée Bourdelle

3 Émile-Antoine Bourdelle
Rodin at work 1910
Paris, Musée Bourdelle

4 Émile-Antoine Bourdelle
Apollo and the Muses 1912
Paris, relief on façade
of the Théâtre des Champs-Élysées
(*overleaf*)

75 Émile-Antoine Bourdelle
    Ingres 1908
    Paris, Musée Bourdelle

76 Émile-Antoine Bourdelle
    Hand of warrior 1909
    Paris, Musée Bourdelle

177 Émile-Antoine Bourdelle
Le fruit 1911
Paris, Musée Bourdelle

178 Émile-Antoine Bourdelle
Little sculptress resting 1905–6
Paris, Musée Bourdelle

179 Charles Despiau
Paulette 1910
Paris, Musée National
d'Art Moderne

180 Charles Despiau
Eve 1925
Paris, Musée National
d'Art Moderne

181 Henri Matisse
The slave 1900–3
New York, Museum of Modern
Mr and Mrs Sam Salz Fund

182 Henri Matisse
Copy of Barye's jaguar 1899–1901
Switzerland,
Theodore Ahrenberg Collection
(*see* 73)

183 Henri Matisse
Reclining nude III 1929
Baltimore Museum of Art
Cone Collection
(*top right*)

184 Henri Matisse
La Serpentine 1909
New York, Museum of Modern
Gift of Abby Aldrich Rockefeller

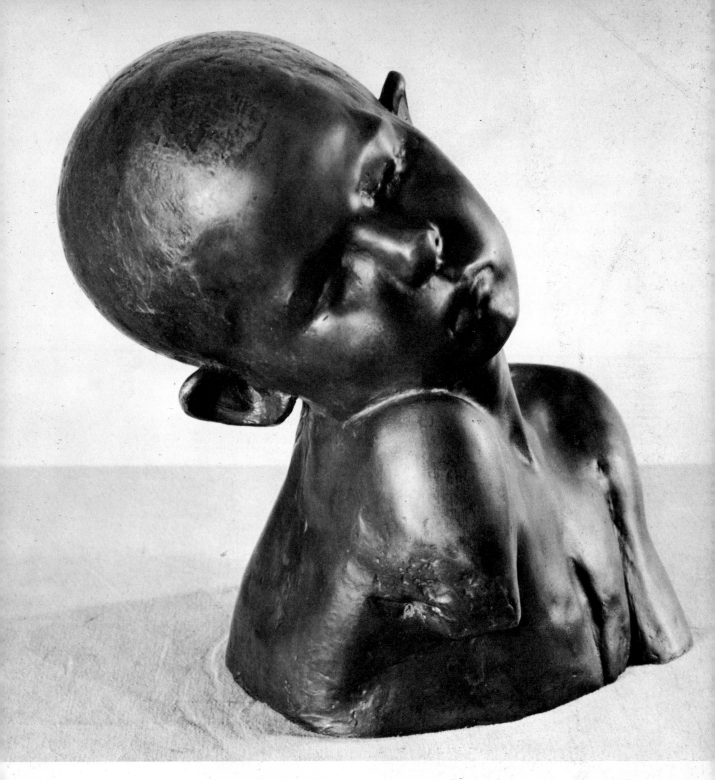

185 Henri Matisse
Tiaré with necklace 1930
Baltimore Museum of Art
Cone Collection

186 Constantin Brancusi
Head of boy 1907
New York, Marlborough-
Gerson Gallery

7 Constantin Brancusi
The kiss
(*tomb of Tanosa Gassevskaia*) 1910
Paris, Cimetière de Montparnasse

8 Constantin Brancusi
The cock 1941
Paris, Musée National d'Art Moderne

189 Constantin Brancusi
Torso of a young man 1922
Philadelphia Museum of Art
Louise and Walter Arensberg
Collection

190 Constantin Brancusi
Torso of a young girl 1922
Philadelphia Museum of Art
A. E. Gallatin Collection

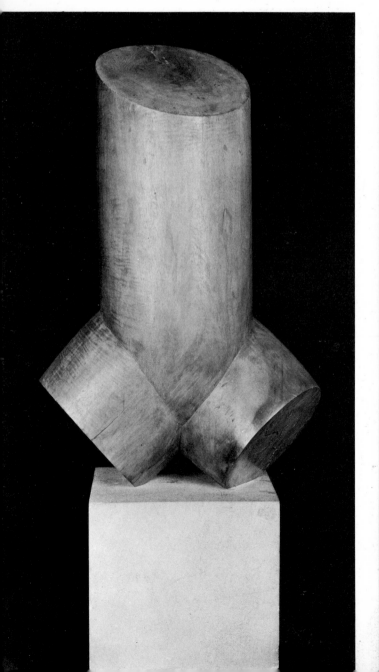

191 Constantin Brancusi
Bird in space 1940
Venice, Peggy Guggenheim
Collection

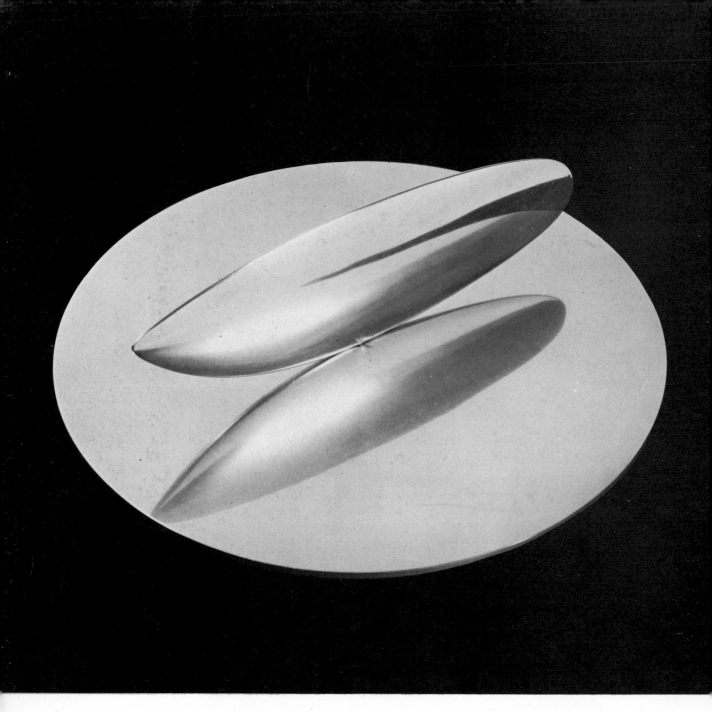

192 Constantin Brancusi
The fish 1924
Boston, Mass., Museum of Fine Arts

93 Constantin Brancusi
The newborn 1920
New York, Museum of Modern Art
Acquired through Lillie P. Bliss Bequest

194 Constantin Brancusi
King of Kings 1937
New York, Solomon
R. Guggenheim Museum

195 Henri Gaudier-Brzeska
The imp 1914
London, Tate Gallery

196 Amedeo Modigliani
Head of a young girl 1913
Seattle Art Museum
Eugene Fuller Memorial Collection

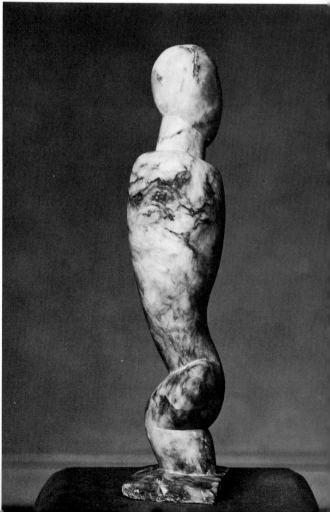

197 Amedeo Modigliani
Full-length figure 1908
New York
Gustave Schindler Collection

198 & 199 Amedeo Modigliani
Caryatid c. 1914
New York, Museum of Modern Art
Mrs Simon Guggenheim Fund

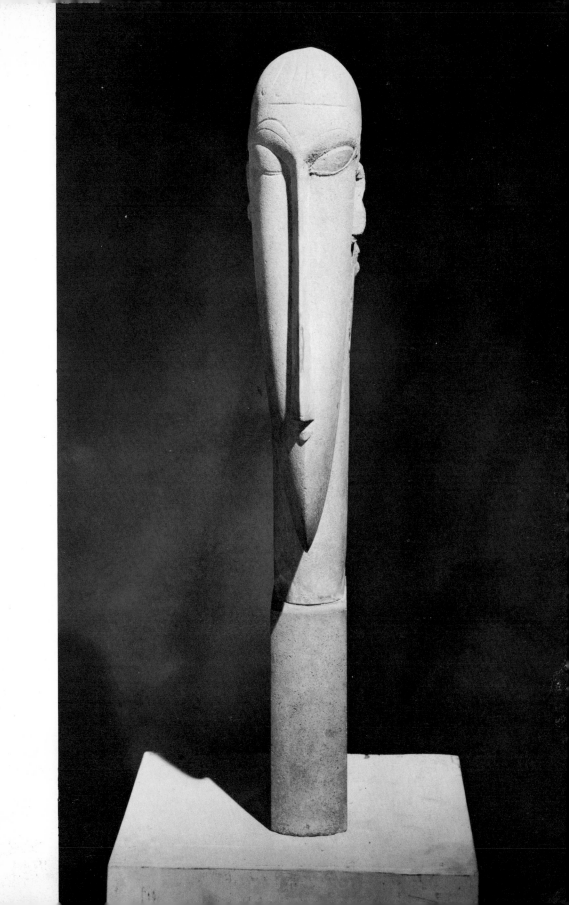

200 Amedeo Modigliani
Head 1914
New York, Perls Galleries

201 Amedeo Modigliani
Head 1910–13
London, Tate Gallery

202 Wilhelm Lehmbruck
Standing youth 1913
New York, Museum of Modern Art
Gift of Abby Aldrich Rockefeller

203 Georges Minne
St John 1895
Ghent, Musée des Beaux-Arts

204 Wilhelm Lehmbruck
Kneeling woman 1911
New York, Museum of Modern Art
Abby Aldrich Rockefeller Fund

205 Wilhelm Lehmbruck
Female torso 1918
Duisburg, Wilhelm Lehmbruck Museum
(*below*)

206 Moissej Kogan
Female figure 1933
Rotterdam, Museum Boymans-
van Beuningen (*right*)

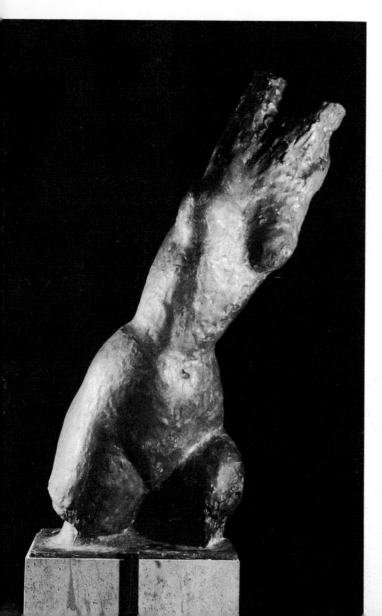

207 Ernst Barlach
   Cleopatra 1904
   Hamburg, H. F. Reemtsma
   Collection

208 Ernst Barlach
   The ascetic 1925
   Hamburg, H. F. Reemtsma
   Collection

209 Ernst Barlach
Figures from the Church of St Catherine 1930–
Lübeck

10 Käthe Kollwitz
Self-portrait 1926–36
Berlin, Dr Hans Kollwitz
Collection

11 Ernst Kirchner
The two friends 1925–6
Basle, Kunstmuseum

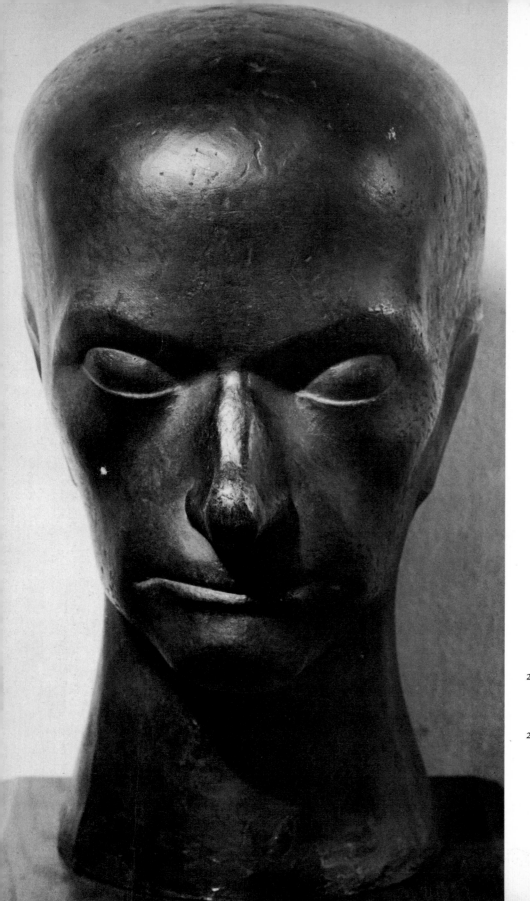

212 Raymond Duchamp-Villon
Baudelaire 1911
New York, Museum of Modern ▲

213 Sir Jacob Epstein
Portrait of Dolores 1923
London, Lady Epstein Collection

214 Sir Jacob Epstein
Tomb of Oscar Wilde 1912
Paris, Cimetière du Père Lachaise

215 Sir Jacob Epstein
Social consciousness 1951–2
Philadelphia Museum of Art
Ellen P. Samuel Memorial
Fairmount Park Art Association

216 & 217 Arturo Martini
The prostitute 1909–13
Venice, Ca' Pesaro

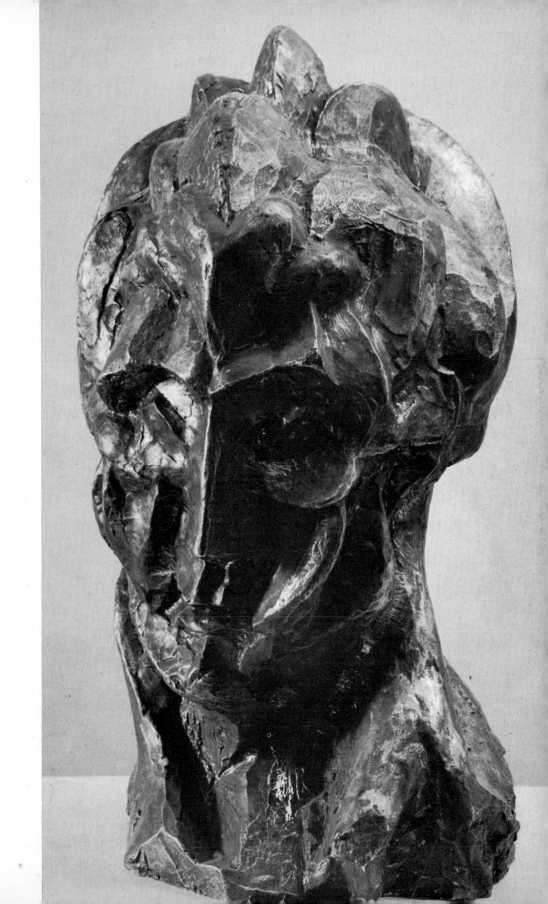

218 Pablo Picasso
The jester 1905
Paris, Galerie Louise Leiris

219 Pablo Picasso
Head of a woman 1909–10
Paris, Galerie Berggruen

220 Umberto Boccioni
The mother 1912
Birmingham, Mich.
Mr and Mrs Harry Lewis
Winston Collection

221 Umberto Boccioni
Unique forms of continuity in space 1913
Milan, Gianni Mattioli Collection

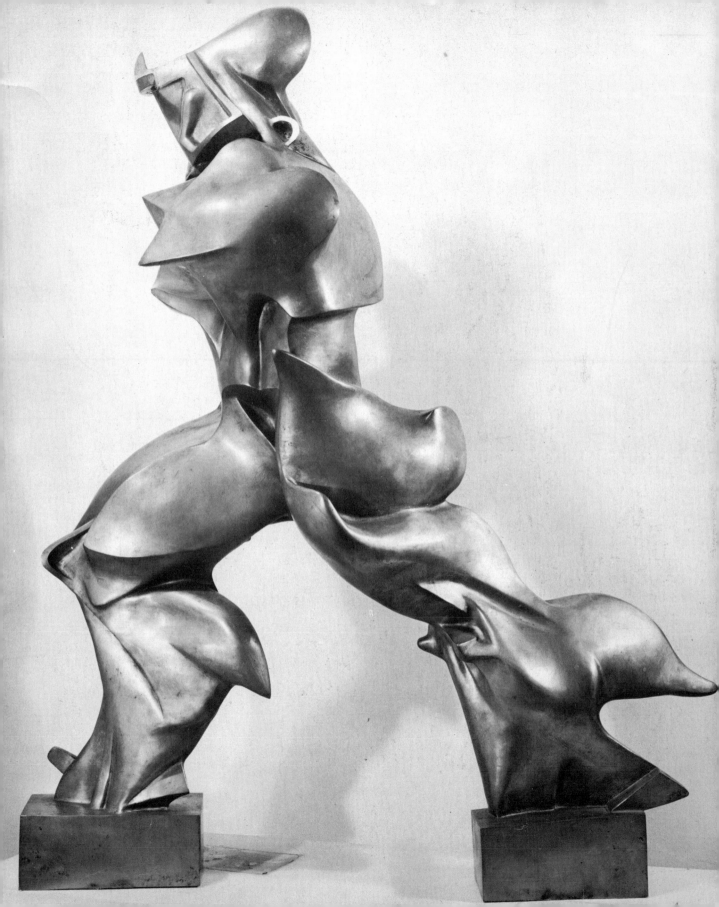

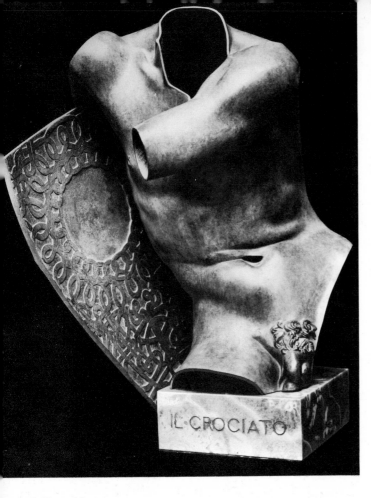

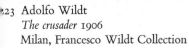

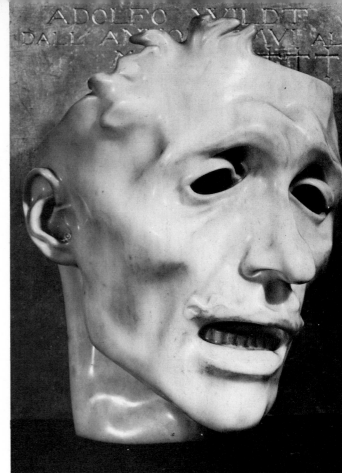

223 Adolfo Wildt
The crusader 1906
Milan, Francesco Wildt Collection

224 Adolfo Wildt
Self-portrait 1908
Florence, Galleria degli Uffizi

25 Giacomo Balla
Boccioni's fist – lines of force 1915
Rome, Luce Balla Collection
(*left*)

26 Raymond Duchamp–Villon
The horse 1914
New York, Museum of Modern Art
Van Gogh Purchase Fund
(*below*)

27 Jacques Lipchitz
Man with mandolin 1917
New Haven, Conn., Yale University
Art Gallery
Société Anonyme Collection

228 Jacques Lipchitz
Sailor with guitar 1914
Philadelphia Museum of Art

229 Jacques Lipchitz
Pierrot escaping 1927
Zürich, Kunsthaus

230 Henri Laurens
Man with a pipe 1919
Paris, Galerie Louise Leiris

231 Henri Laurens
Red and black sheet iron 1914
Paris, Mme Maurice
Raynal Collection

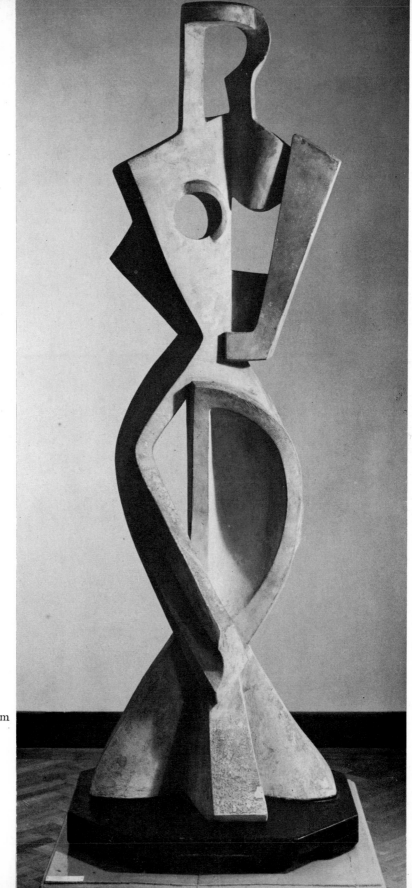

2 Henri Laurens
Tomb of the artist and his wife
(designed 1941)
Paris, Cimetière de Montparnasse

3 Alexander Archipenko
Standing figure 1920
Darmstadt, Hessisches Landesmuseum

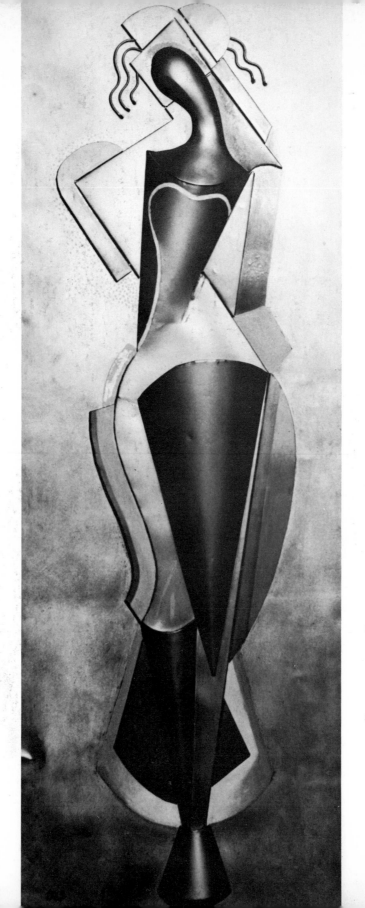

234 Alexander Archipenko
The metal lady 1923
New Haven, Conn., Yale
University Art Gallery
Société Anonyme Collection

235 Alexander Archipenko
Boxing match 1935
Venice, Peggy Guggenheim
Collection

236 Ossip Zadkine
*Monument – the destroyed city
of Rotterdam* 1953–4
Rotterdam, Blaak, Schiedamse D

237 Ossip Zadkine
Mother and child c. 1918
New York, Joseph H.
Hirshhorn Collection

238 Elie Nadelman
Standing bull 1915
New York, Museum of Modern Art
Gift of Mrs Elie Nadelman

239 Elie Nadelman
Woman at the piano c. 1917
New York, Museum of Modern Art
Philip L. Goodwin Collection

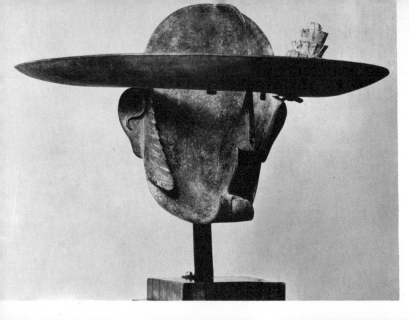

240 Pablo Gargallo
Picador 1928
New York, Museum of Modern Art
Gift of A. Conger Goodyear

241 Georges Braque
Woman 1920
Paris, Galerie Louise Leiris

242 Laszlo Moholy-Nagy
Mobile sculpture 1943
Chicago, Mrs Morton Zurcher
Collection

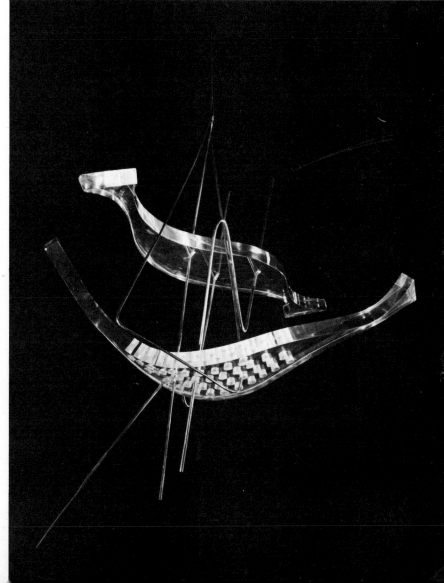

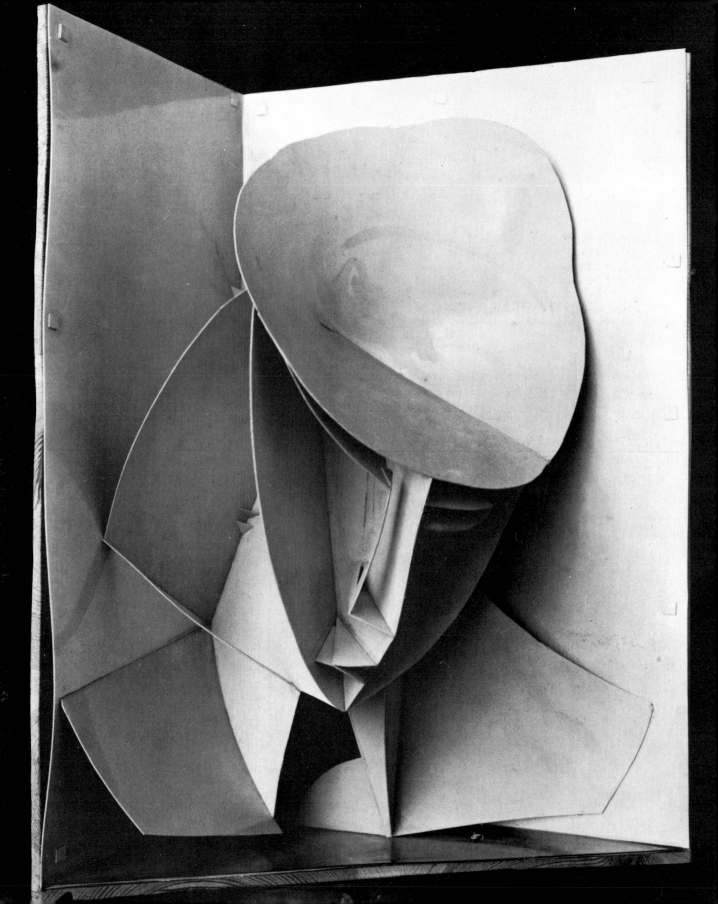

43 Naum Gabo
Head of a woman 1916–17
Middlebury, Conn., the artist's collection

44 Antoine Pevsner
Torso 1924–6
New York, Museum of Modern Art
Katherine S. Dreier Bequest

245 Naum Gabo
*Monument for an institute
of physics and mathematics* 1920
U.S.S.R.

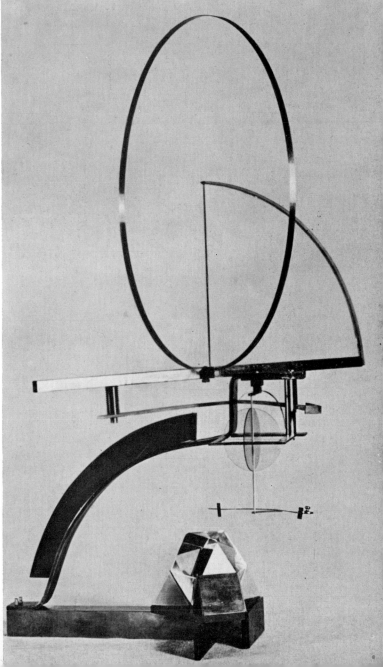

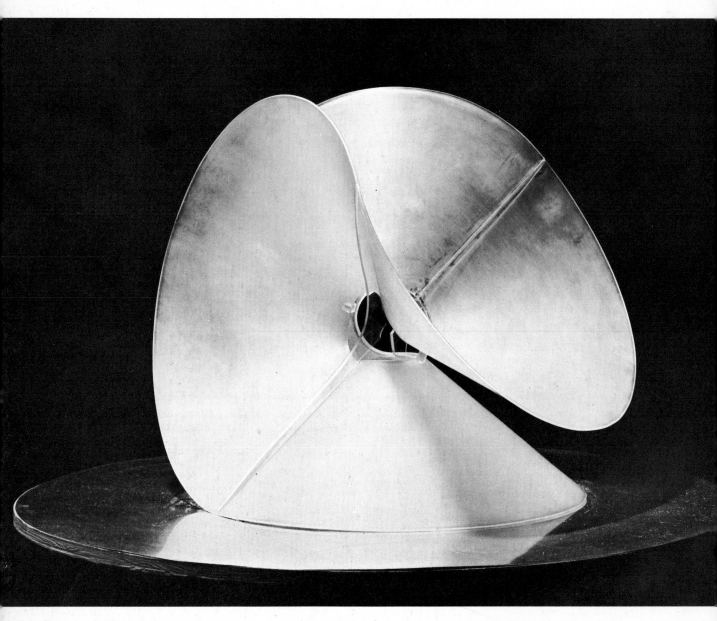

246 Naum Gabo
Translucent variations on a spheric theme 1937
Middlebury, Conn., the artist's collection

247 Naum Gabo
Linear construction No. 2 1942–3
Middlebury, Conn., Miriam Gabo
Collection

248 Naum Gabo
Construction in space 1955–7
Rotterdam, N.V. Magazijn De
Bijenkorf

249 Antoine Pevsner
World construction 1947
Paris, Musée National
d'Art Moderne

250 Georges Vantongerloo
Equation in chrome 1935
Basle, Kunstmuseum
Emanuel Hoffman-Stiftung

251 Oskar Schlemmer
Abstract figure 1921
Stuttgart
Frau Tut Schlemmer Collection

252 Georges Vantongerloo
Construction in an inscribed
and circumscribed square of a mile 1924
Venice, Peggy Guggenheim Collection

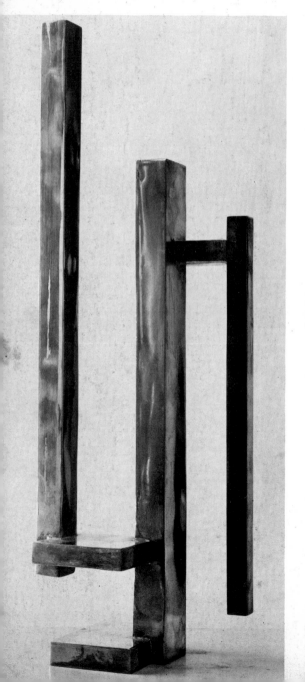

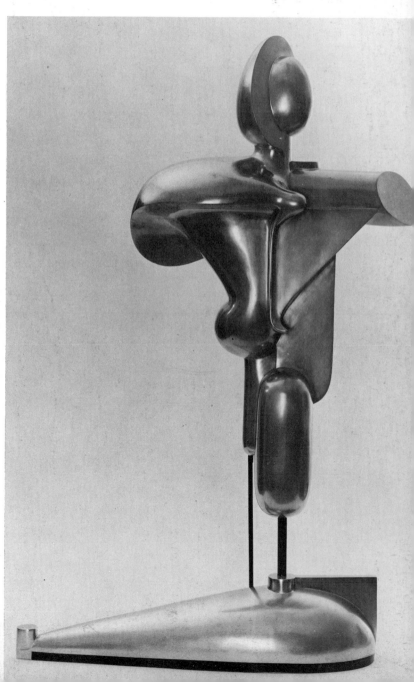

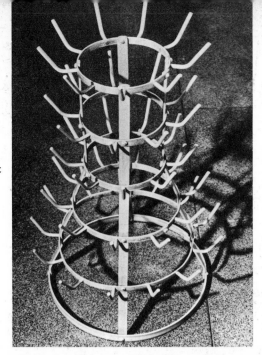

257 Pablo Picasso
Glass of absinth 1919
New York, Museum of Modern Art
Gift of Mrs Louise Smith

258 Marcel Duchamp
Bottlerack 1914
Paris, Man Ray Collection

259 Marcel Duchamp
Ready-made: Why not sneeze,
Rrose Sélavy? 1921
Philadelphia Museum of Art
Louise and Walter Arensberg
Collection

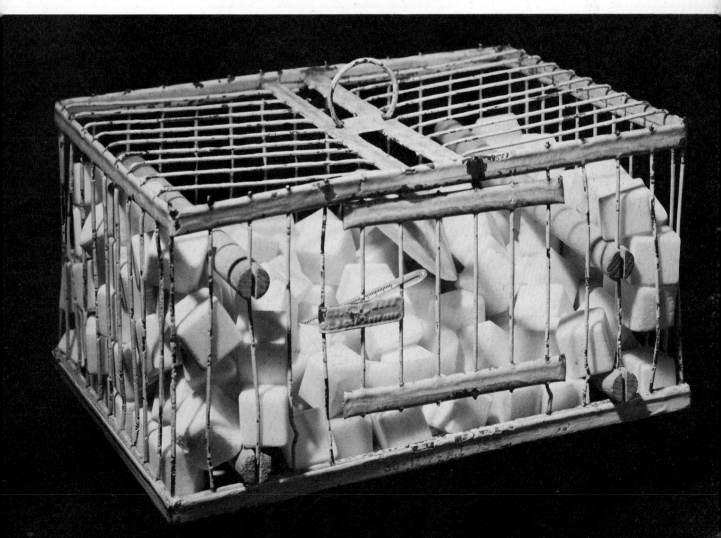

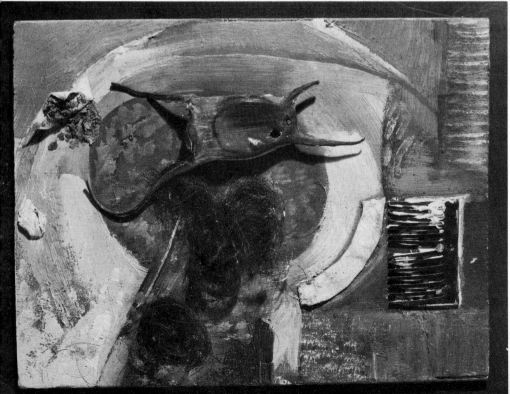

260 Meret Oppenheim
Fur-covered cup, plate and spoon 193[
New York, Museum of Modern [

261 Kurt Schwitters
Mermaid's purse 1942–5
London, Lord's Gallery

262 Laurence Vail
A quoi rêvent les jeunes filles 1962
Venice, Peggy Guggenheim
Collection

263 Lee Bontecou
Untitled 1961
New York, Whitney Museum of
American Art
(*left*)

264 Joseph Cornell
Pharmacy 1942–5
Venice, Peggy Guggenheim
Collection

265 Joseph Cornell
Bleriot 1954–5
New York, Eleanor Ward Collection

266 Louise Nevelson
Nightscape 1959
Zürich, Gimpel und Hanover Galerie

269 Jean Arp
Silent 1942
Meudon (S.-et-O.), the artist's collection

270 Jean Arp
Ptolemy 1953
New York
Burden Collection

271 Jean Arp
Garland of buds 1936
Venice, Peggy Guggenheim Collection
(*right*)

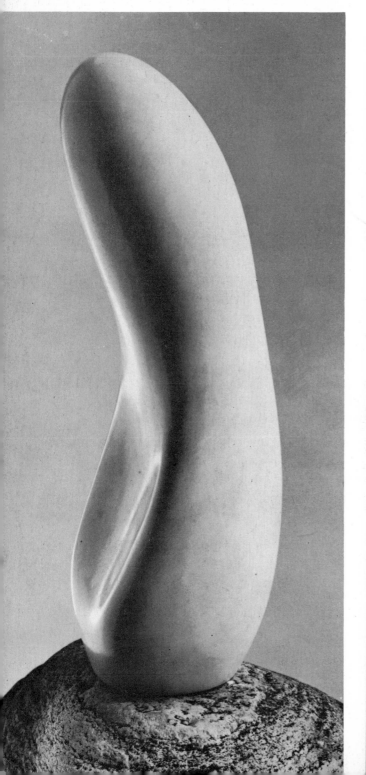

272 Isamu Noguchi
Kouros (in 9 parts) 1944–5
New York, Metropolitan Museum of Art
Fletcher Fund 1953

273 Isamu Noguchi
Hiroshima Bridge (parapets) 1952
Island of Hiroshima,
connecting it with the mainland

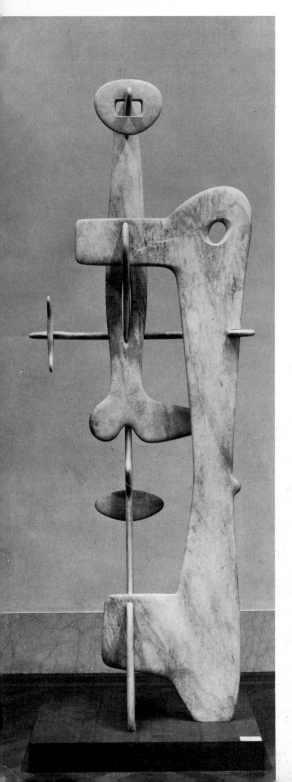

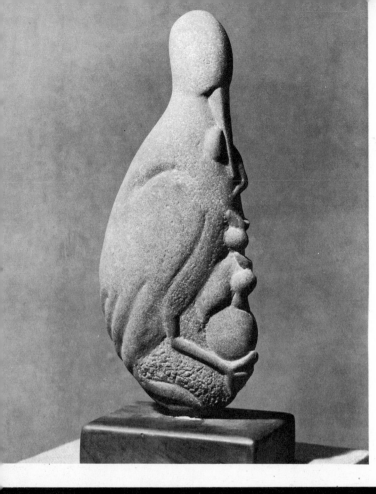

274 John B. Flanagan
Early bird 1941
The Estate of Curt Valentin

275 Fritz Wotruba
Reclining figure 1960
New York, Marlborough-Gerson Gallery

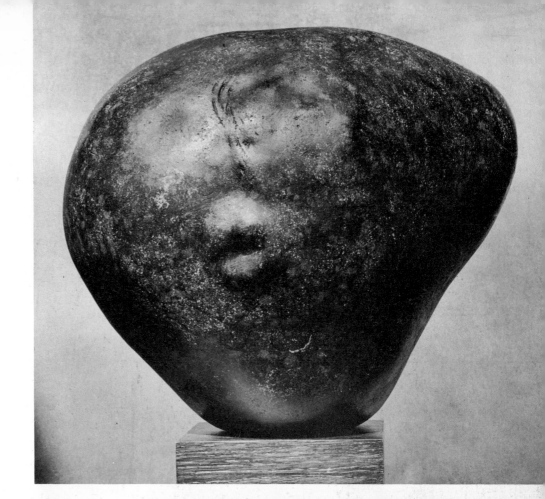

279 Alberto Giacometti
Invisible object
(*vide, maintenant le vide*) *c.* 1934–5
Saint-Paul-de-Vence,
Maeght Foundation

280 Alberto Giacometti
Female figure 1946–7
Venice, Peggy Guggenheim
Collection

281 Alberto Giacometti
Woman with her throat cut 1949
New York, Museum of
Modern Art

282 Alberto Giacometti
People in the piazza 1948–9
Basle, Kunstmuseum
Emanuel Hoffman-Stiftung

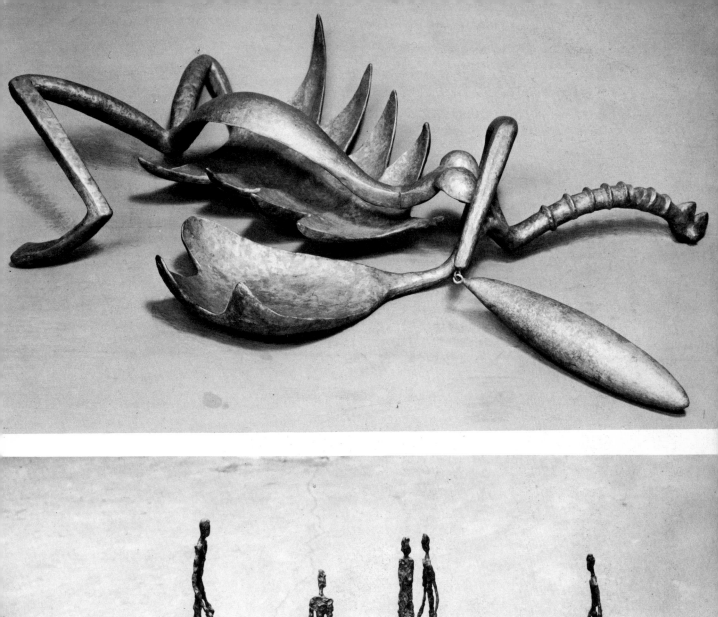

283 Alberto Giacometti
Portrait of Diego 1954
Saint-Paul-de-Vence, Maeght
Foundation

284 Max Ernst
Lunar asparagus 1935
New York
Museum of Modern Art

285 Max Ernst
The king playing with the queen 195
New York
Museum of Modern Art
Gift of Mr and Mrs John de Men

286 Max Ernst
Streets of Athens 1960
Venice, Peggy Guggenheim
Collection

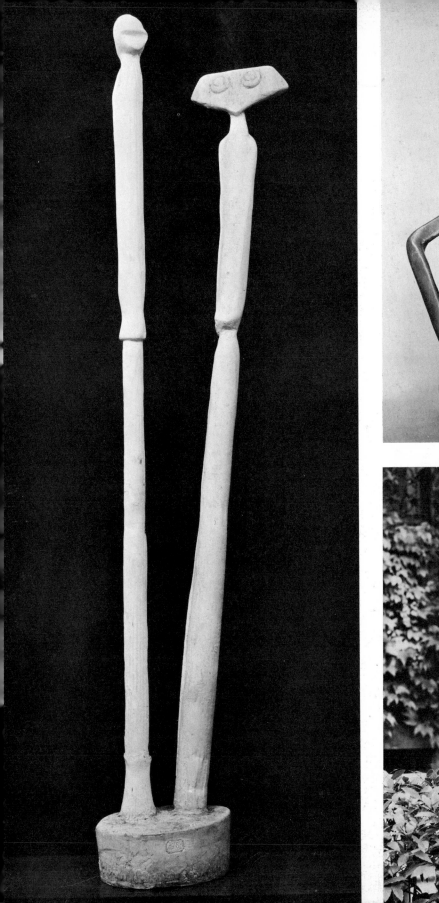

287 Jacques Lipchitz
Figure 1926–30
Hudson, N.Y., the artist's collectio

288 Jacques Lipchitz
Mother and child II 1941–5
New York, Museum of Modern A
Mrs Simon Guggenheim Fund

289 Jacques Lipchitz
Blossoming 1941–2
New York, Museum of Modern Art

290 Joan Miró
Woman 1950
Paris, Galerie Maeght (*right*)

291 Jacques Lipchitz
Here are the fruits and the flowers 1955–6
New York, Marlborough-Gerson Gallery

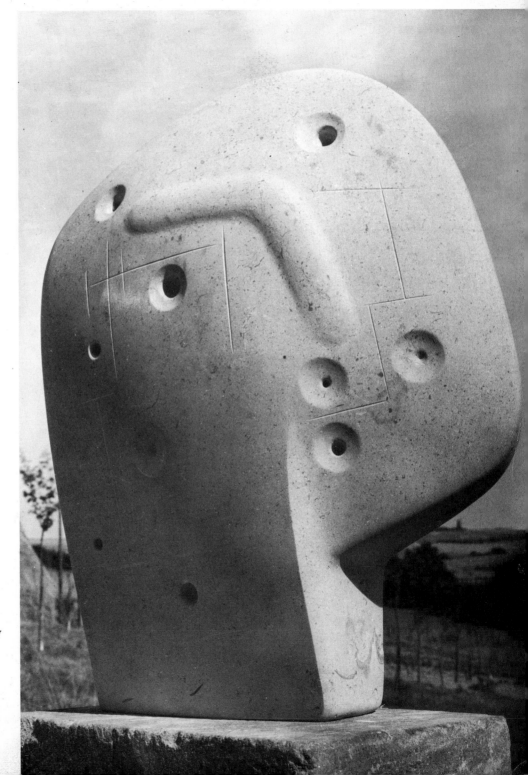

292 Henry Moore
Bird basket 1939
Private collection

293 Henry Moore
Head 1937
New York, Martha Jackson Gallery

294 Henry Moore
The warrior 1953–4
Minneapolis Institute of Arts
Gift of John Cowles

295 Henry Moore
King and queen 1952–3
Antwerp, Middelheim Open
Air Museum

296 Henry Moore
Head and helmet 1950
Venice, Ca' Pesaro

297 Barbara Hepworth
Large and small forms 1945
Private collection

298 Kenneth Armitage
The family going for a walk 1951
Private collection

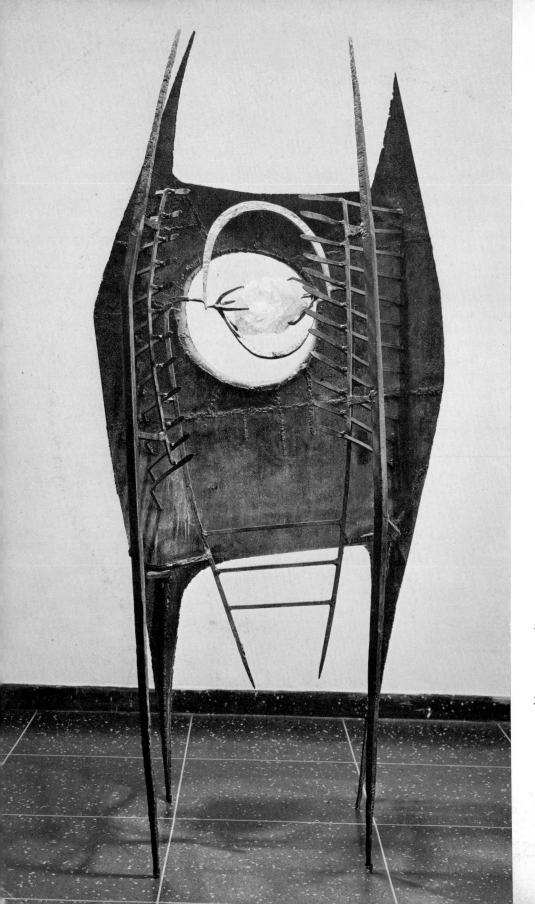

299 Lynn Chadwick
Inner eye 1962
New York, Museum of Modern
A. Conger Goodyear Fund

300 Alexander Calder
Mobile 1934
Philadelphia Museum of Art
Louise and Walter Arensberg
Collection

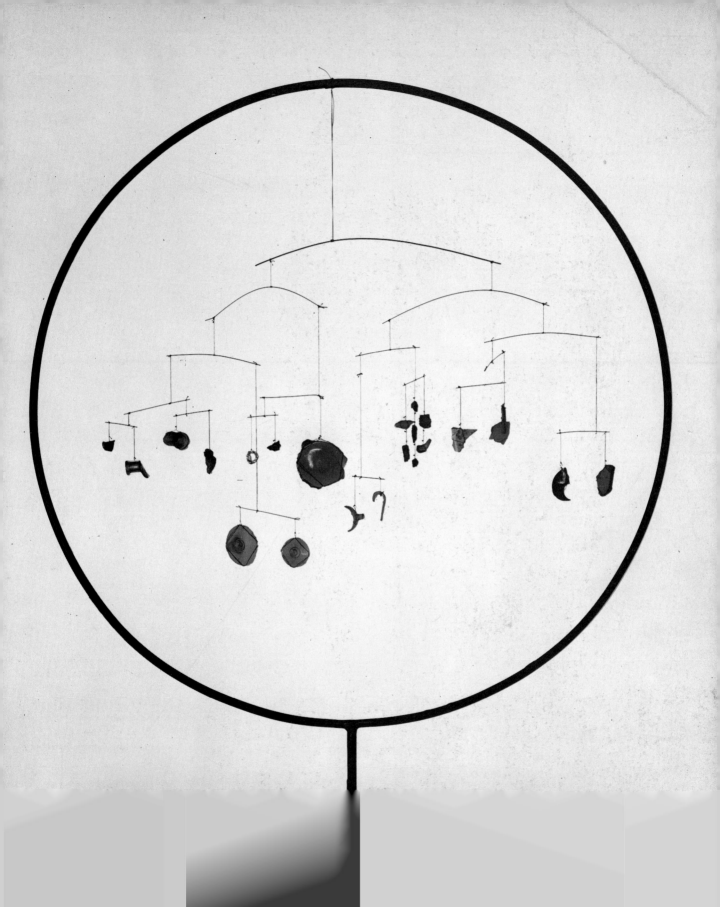

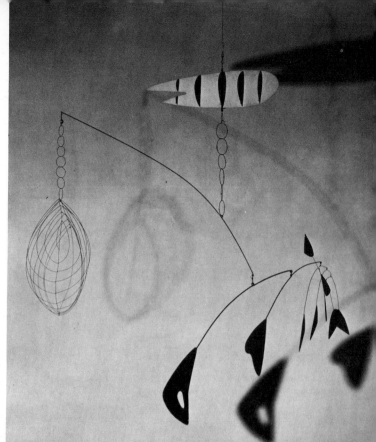

301 Alexander Calder
   Josephine Baker 1926
   New York, Perls Galleries

302 Alexander Calder
   Lobster trap and fish tail 1939
   New York, Museum of Modern Art
   Gift of the Advisory Committee (*above*)

303 Alexander Calder
   Whale 1937
   New York, Museum of Modern Art
   Gift of the artist

304 Germain Richier
The bat-man 1946
Hartford, Conn., Wadsworth Atheneum
Collection

305 Richard Lippold
The spirit vine 1957
Pauillac, Gironde
Château Mouton-Rothschild

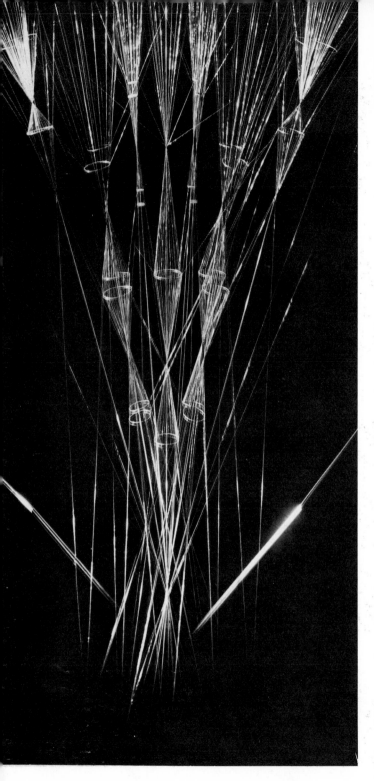

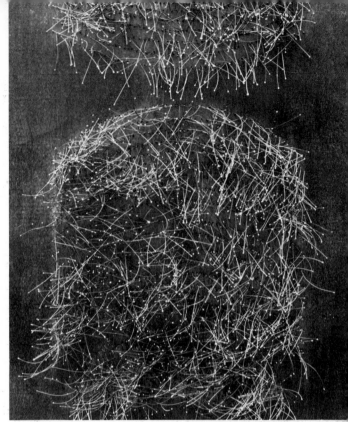

306 Pol Bury
Punctuation 1963
New York, Lefebre Gallery
(*far right, top*)

307 Vassilakis Takis
Tele-sculpture 1959
Private collection

308 Julio Gonzalez
Little classic head 1910–14
Paris, Hans Hartung Collection

309 Eduardo Chillida
Enclume de Rêve No. 10 1962
Basle, Kunstmuseum
Emanuel Hoffman-Stiftung (*right*)

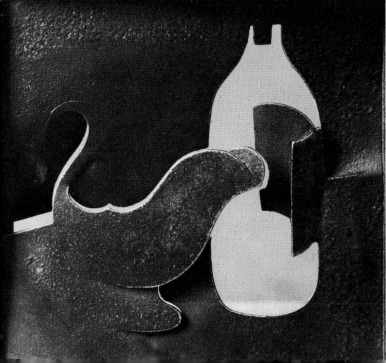

310 Julio Gonzalez
Woman combing her hair 1936
New York, Museum of Modern Art
Mrs Simon Guggenheim Fund (*above*)

311 Julio Gonzalez
Still life c. 1927–9
Paris, Mme Roberta Gonzalez Collection

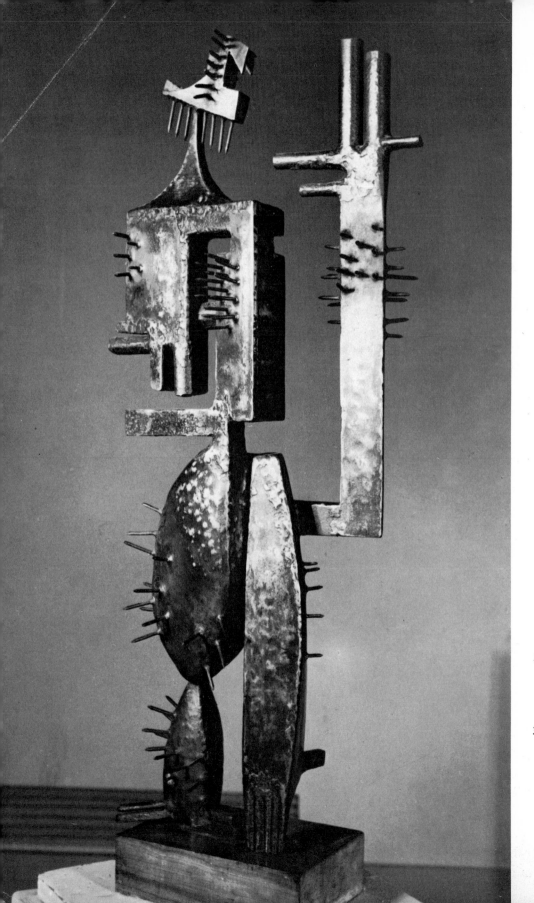

312 Julio Gonzalez
Cactus-man No 1 1939–40
Paris, Mme Roberta Gonzalez
Collection

313 Julio Gonzalez
Montserrat 1937
Amsterdam, Stedelijk Museum

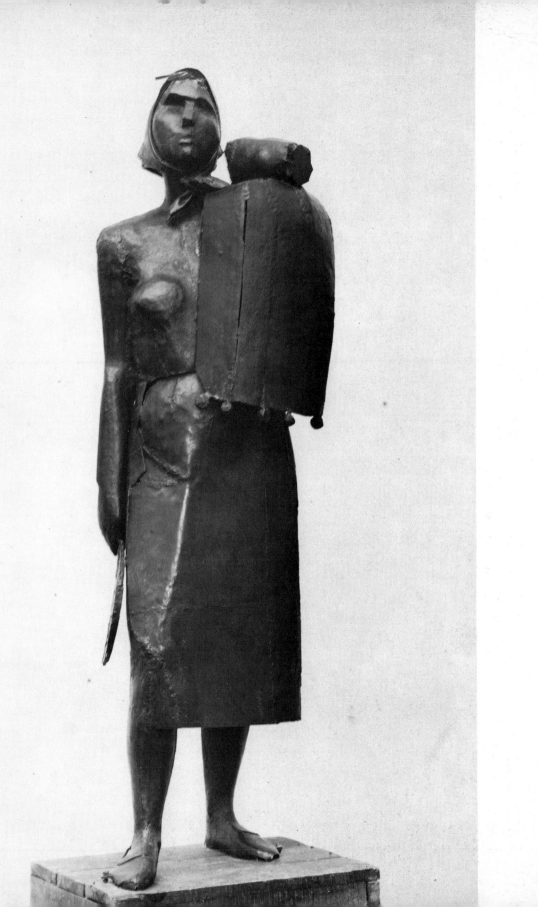

314 Arturo Martini
Woman at the window 1941
Rome, Galleria Nazionale
d'Arte Moderna

315 Arturo Martini
The dream 1931
Acqui-Terme, Ottolenghi Collection

316 Marino Marini
Popolo 1929
Milan, the artist's collection

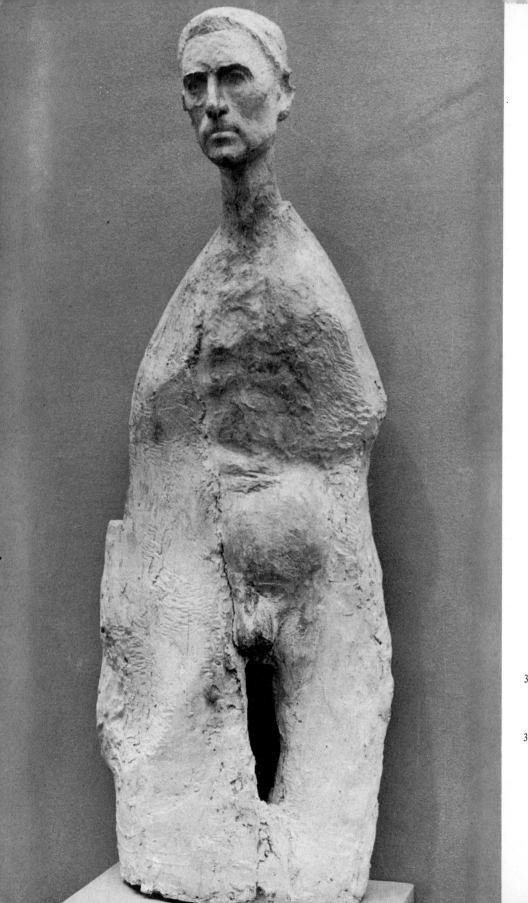

317 Marino Marini
Arcangelo 1943
Basle, Kunstmuseum

318 Marino Marini
Igor Stravinsky 1951
Minneapolis Institute of Arts

319 Marino Marini
Venus 1938
Milan, private collection

320 Marino Marini
The miracle (horse and rider) 1959–6
Zürich, Kunsthaus

321 Giacomo Manzù
Grande cardinale 1955
Venice, Ca' Pesaro

322 Giacomo Manzù
Doors of St Peter's
commissioned
1952, cast 1963
Rome

327 Pablo Picasso
Skull 1944
The artist's collection

328 Pablo Picasso
Shepherd holding a lamb 1944
Philadelphia Museum of Art
R. Sturgis Ingersoll Collection

329 Pablo Picasso
Baboon and young 1951
New York
Museum of Modern Art
Mrs Simon Guggenheim Fund

330 Pablo Picasso
Owl 1953
The Estate of Curt Valentin

331 David Smith
The letter 1950
Utica, N.Y., Munson Williams
Proctor Institute

332 Mary Callery
Fables of La Fontaine 1954
New York, Public School No. 34

333 Zoltán Kemény
Spirit converter 1963
Zürich, the artist's collection

334 David Smith
Head 1938
New York, Museum of
Modern Art

335 Mirko Basaldella
Gates of the Fosse Ardeatine 1950
Rome

336 François Stähly
Fountain 1963
St Gallen, Handelshochschule

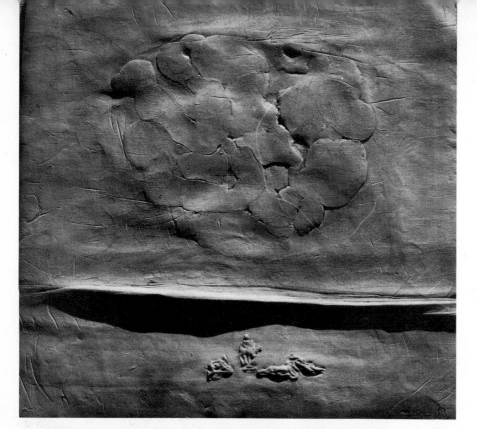

337 Constantino Nivola
Gods and humans 1964
New York, Byron Gallery

338 Alicia Penalba
Sculptures in concrete 1963
St Gallen, Handelshochschule

339 Theodore Roszak
Chrysalis 1936–7
New York, the artist's collection

340 Theodore Roszak
Skylark 1950–1
New York, Pierre Matisse Gallery

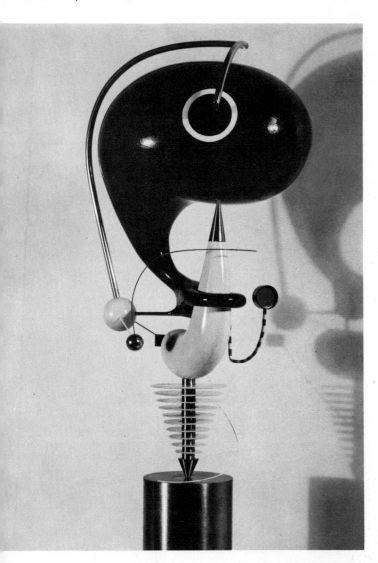

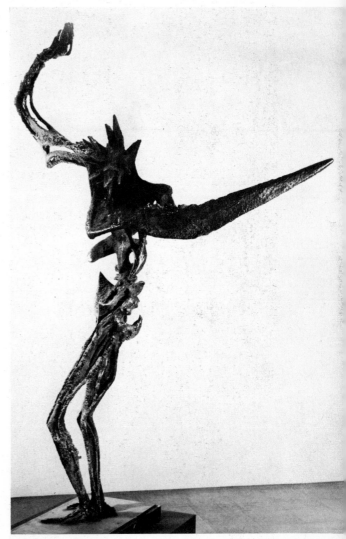

341 John Chamberlain
Madame Moon 1964
Los Angeles, Robert A. Rowan
Collection

342 Jasper Johns
Light bulb 1960
Los Angeles
Irving Blum Collection

343 Richard Stankiewicz
Untitled 1961
Meriden, Conn., Mr and Mrs Burton
Tremaine Collection

344 Robert Rauschenberg
The bed 1955
New York, Leo Castelli Gallery

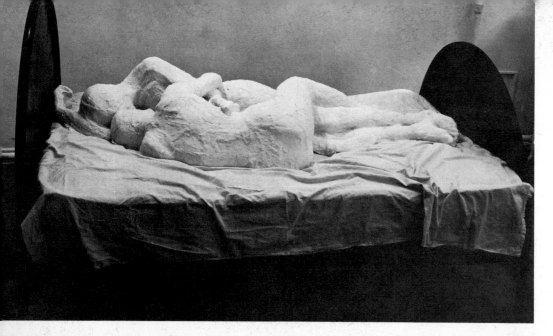

345 George Segal
Sleeping Lovers 1963
Winnetka, Ill., Robert Mayer
Collection

346 Aristide Croisy
Le nid 1882
Paris, Musée de Montbrison

347 & 348 Félix Desruelles
Monument to four hostages,
original 1924,
destroyed 1941, reconstructed
1960
Lille, Boulevards Vauban
et Liberté

349 Jean Tinguely
Self-destroying machine 1960
New York, Museum of
Modern Art
(overleaf)

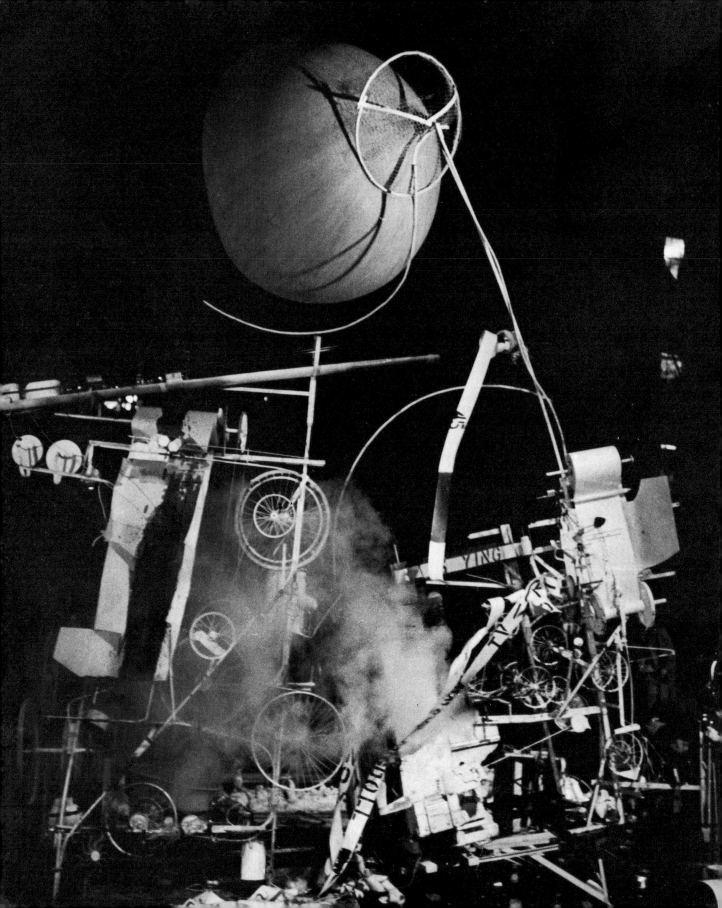

NOTES ON THE COLOUR PLATES

Measurements are given in the order height, width, depth, except where indicated otherwise.

    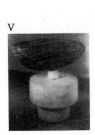   

I   II   III   IV   V   VI   VII   VIII

ANTONIO CANOVA

I   *Meekness (Mansuetudine)* 1783 terracotta 13 × 11 × 9 cm.
Possagno, Gipsoteca Canoviana
The process by which Canova achieved the tranquillity of compositions from which every anecdotal incident has been sheared away was an arduous one of constant simplification and the subtracting of everything extraneous. This first sketch for the tomb of Clement XIV shows how intuitively Canova worked. 'Clay is life,' he said, 'plaster is death and marble is the resurrection.'

JEAN-BAPTISTE CARPEAUX

II   *Neapolitan fisherboy* 1863 marble 107 × 42 × 47 cm.
Washington, D.C., National Gallery of Art, Samuel H. Kress Collection
Rude's *Fisherboy* (58) in its fresh realism was much imitated and copied, especially in small decorative bronzes which were highly marketable. Carpeaux alone was capable of taking the motif and shedding all of Rude's laborious naturalism to create a work of unparalleled vibrancy.

AUGUSTE RODIN

III   *La Défense* 1878 bronze 109 cm.
Paris, Musée Rodin
This daring, explosive composition was never to be surpassed, even by Rodin himself. Though a reminiscence of Rude's *Marseillaise* (60) still lingers, the way this figure shoots out of the void into which the slain soldier is sinking is totally new. Still more important, the flashing, febrile reflections on the agitated surface give the sculpture a unity of dramatic expression never before achieved.

EDGAR DEGAS

IV   *The little ballet-dancer, 14 years old* 1880 bronze; skirt, muslin; hair-ribbon, satin 99 cm. London, Tate Gallery
In a shocking and daring rebellion against Aristotelian aesthetics, Degas freely mixed elements of the real world (slippers, dress and ribbon) with his sculpture, thus breaking down the barriers which divide art and daily, mortal reality. But our recognition of the interplay between the real and the imaginary only serves to make the imaginary world more real. The arrogant pose, and Degas's insistence on giving us the age of his subject, intimates the whole dilemma of this creature's existence: caught in a moment in which she is not dancing, she is reduced to a graceless, lonesome and irrelevant object.

CONSTANTIN BRANCUSI

V   *Fish* 1930 blue-green marble 53 × 180 cm.
New York, Museum of Modern Art. Acquired through the Lillie P. Bliss Bequest
Material and subject interpenetrate in this evocation not only of the smooth swiftness of the fish but also of his watery habitation which streams past him.

ALEXANDER CALDER

VI   *Red petals* 1942 aluminium 279 cm.
Chicago, the Arts Club
Sheet iron and wire are here transformed into resilient boughs, stems and leaves. The harmony of these mobiles is carefully calculated by the artist to resolve itself no matter what new and unforeseeable relationships are produced by the motion of the various parts. In anticipation of his later stabiles (303), Calder effectively uses the resiliently rearing base as part of his sculpture.

MARCEL DUCHAMP

VII   *The large glass (The bride stripped bare by her bachelors, even)* 1915–25 287 × 176 cm.
Philadelphia Museum of Art, Louise and Walter Arensberg Collection
Begun as a highly intellectual proposition, finished by an accidental breakage which incorporated the irruption of the unforeseeable, this work defies all categories, being at once painting, architectural element and sculpture. It also represents the ultimate conclusion of the modern urge to integrate the dimensions of time and space into art since it can never be seen by itself but always includes objects and spaces seen *through* it.

RICHARD LIPPOLD

VIII   *Variations within a sphere No. 10. The sun* 1953–6 gold-filled wire 335 × 56 × 168 cm.
New York, Metropolitan Museum of Art, Fletcher Fund 1956
A complicated, airy suspension of thinnest golden wire graphs the expanding rays of sun as they scatter through a space which they define and enliven. In Lippold, as in many other contemporary American sculptors, the unsubstantial and the densely physical are completely interdependent; as here glittering light and airy motion are fused with gold wire polished to perfection.

305

NOTES ON THE MONOCHROME ILLUSTRATIONS

Measurements are given in the order height, width, depth, except where indicated otherwise.

JEAN-ANTOINE HOUDON
b. Versailles 1741 – d. Paris 1828
1   *S. Bruno* 1766 marble
Rome, Sta Maria degli Angeli
Several elements relate this figure to late-Baroque traditions: the turned position of the saint within the niche, the deliberate displacement of major vertical axes out of true centre, the very dramatic ponderation of sleeves and folds which agitate the silhouette and the poignant intensity of the closed eyes. The moral severity, however, the lack of histrionic gesture and, above all, the rigorous restraint of emotion make of this sculpture the first monumental work of eighteenth-century Neoclassicism.

ANTONIO CANOVA
b. Possagno (Italy) 1757 – d. Venice 1822
2   *Daedalus and Icarus* 1779 marble 170 × 95 × 92 cm.
Venice, Museo Correr
Canova's early work before his first visit to Rome bears the clear imprint of Baroque sculpture in its agitated, energetic movement. The outline of the group is continually broken as the figures lean towards or away from each other. The modelling is naturalistic and shows a very sure hand in the treatment of muscles in motion and in the comparison of youthful and ageing flesh.

3   *Briseis surrendered to the heralds of Agamemnon* 1790 plaster 110 × 210 cm.
Possagno, Gipsoteca Canoviana
Relief was the most natural mode of Neoclassic expression because its limited depth and shallow modelling tended to reduce effusive dramatics, and because its closed silhouette emphasized the linear element. Neoclassic artists also revolutionized the concept of relief-cutting by associating it with the Classic art of cameo-carving: the ground of the relief is no longer a matrix from which the figures grow but a neutral, abstract void which isolates each figure.

4   *Cupid and Psyche* 1793 plaster 135 × 151 × 81 cm.
New York, Metropolitan Museum of Art, gift of Isador Strauss, 1905
The erotic myths of Greece provided the themes most germane to Canova's talent. When dealing with a subject combining corporeal and spiritual rapture, he resolved the conflict between Classic stylization and overt realism very harmoniously. The intricate, concentric composition frames the moment of suspense before the embrace.

5   *Tomb of Clement XIV* 1784–7 marble
Rome, SS. Apostoli
With the unveiling of his first major work in Rome, Canova became 'king' of the European art world. Inspired by Neoclassic theories of impassive serenity, the allegorical figures designed by the sculptor are motionless and totally isolated from one another. The stark gesture of Pope Clement, in contrast to the immobile allegories, adds a note of movement reminiscent of David's contemporary canvases.

6   *Monument to Angelo Emo* 1792–5 marble
Venice, Museo Storico Navale
Combining a portrait bust and allegorical figures is a standard device in monumental tomb sculpture. But before Canova's day the portrait and the allegory were always subjected to the same stylistic idiom. Here the gulf which divides the spiritual world (the stylized allegories) from the corporeal world (the realistic portrait bust) becomes unbridgeable. One language, sober, harsh, objective, is used for the latter; another vocabulary, personal and idealistic dominates the former.

7   *Hebe* 1816 (original 1795–8) marble
Forlì, Pinacoteca
Fastidiously ambiguous (is she rising or descending?), endowed with a last happy echo of eighteenth-century sensuousness, generous in form and in her ample, space-enfolding gesture, this Hebe is free from the romantic yearning characteristic of much Neoclassic statuary. Canova did not dream nostalgically of past graces; he re-created them.

8   *Hercules and Lycas* 1812–15 (original 1796) marble 3·5 m.
Rome, Galleria Nazionale d'Arte Moderna
Stung by critics who denied him the talent for forceful composition, Canova created his most dynamic group which was meant to be seen framed in an archway. His insistence on maintaining the integrity of a closed profile prevented him from expressing movement in terms of Baroque explosiveness. Instead, the tense linearity and the straining against an architectural setting, now unfortunately destroyed, suggest the momentum of pent-up forces which remain perpetually enchained.

9 *Tomb of Clement XIII* 1787–92 marble
Rome, St Peter's
Canova's second papal tomb shows a certain relaxation of discipline in its looser arrangement of figures. But it is important to notice how allegorical personalities have now become symbols rather than individualized embodiments of a concept as they were in the Baroque. Once again, resurrection is not hinted at. Instead of presenting us with a triumphant apotheosis as did Bernini, Canova takes us into a timeless world which is neither Paradise-made-manifest nor our own world represented during a particularly calm moment. Architecturally, the monument is far more compact. Unlike earlier papal tombs, it is not integrated with the niche but remains detached. Structural coherence is achieved by juxtaposition rather than unifying compositional rhythms.

10 *Tomb of Archduchess Maria Christina* 1798–1805 marble 5·8 m.
Vienna, Augustinerkirche
Canova here faced the problem posed by his own preference for figures in the round and the marked prejudice of his contemporary critics in favour of sculptural compositions in relief. Here the figures, moving with measured step, are framed by the pyramid so that we see them as part of their background, in accordance with the principles of relief sculpture. Sculpture, previously frontal (even the most withdrawn and architecture-bound medieval sculptures still face outward), is here made to turn in on itself. More challenging still is Canova's handling of the mock-architectural space. The entrance to the pyramid is rendered very realistically as an actual passageway ready to receive the processional figures in contradiction to the flatness of the pyramid itself. This paradox between space at the centre of the pyramid and lack of space at its perimeter gives a curious ghost-like character to the entire scene. The figures will have to vanish not through the passageway but *into* the church wall, with an implacable onward march which expresses the inevitable progress of all life towards the grave.

11 *Napoleon* 1803–11 bronze
Milan, Palazzo di Brera
In an attempt to revive the ancient *genre* of hero-monuments, Canova produced what is probably the most equivocal of his ambitious works. Recognizably realistic facial features are somewhat unconvincingly blended with an impersonal Classicism in the rest of the figure. The

distance between an age which truly believed in heroes and the contemporary epoch with its conception of man-in-history was too great to be bridged even by a Canova.

12 *Paolina Bonaparte Borghese* (Venus victorious) 1805–8 160 cm. (with bed) × 200 cm.
Rome, Galleria Borghese
The fine grain of Canova's textures, and the equilibrium between calculated elegance and spontaneous animal appeal are here combined to make of this the most widely admired Neoclassical work of sculpture. Canova's ability to juxtapose and resolve opposites is nowhere revealed with greater authority. Ideal type and concrete individuality, goddess and woman, abstract principle of feminine beauty and palpable incarnation of sensual charms – all these paradoxes are blended in this portrait of an intriguingly nonchalant woman.

BERTEL THORVALDSEN
Copenhagen 1770–1844
13 *Ganymede with Jupiter as the eagle* 1817 marble 86 × 107 cm.
Copenhagen, Thorvaldsens Museum
In his *Jason*, Thorvaldsen vied with Polykleitos and produced an archaeologically correct representation of Classical balance. Thorvaldsen's groups, however, go beyond the most severe Greek and Roman demands for frontality. The element of depth is minimized by having the composition resolve itself satisfactorily in two dimensions.

14 *Angel holding a font* 1839 (original 1827) marble 141 cm.
Copenhagen, Church of Our Lady
The smooth, uneventful surfaces of all Thorvaldsen figures give them a peculiarly unreal, stony quality. But the rigorous composition of the kneeling angel with its horizontals, verticals and curving arm is one of rare perfection.

15 *Jason with the Golden Fleece* 1802–3 marble 244 cm.
Copenhagen, Thorvaldsens Museum
The bias towards abstraction and theory in Neoclassic art is powerfully extended by Thorvaldsen. He went far beyond Canova in eradicating any direct points of contact between the observed, or emotionally perceived, world and the work of art. It is an open question whether

16

17

19

18

20

21

22

23

Thorvaldsen deliberately eliminated sensuous response from his work or whether he was congenitally incapable of reacting spontaneously to the physical world.

16　*The Lion of Lucerne* 1819–21 rock 9 m.
　　Lucerne, Gletscherpark
　　Commissioned to commemorate the Swiss Guard of the Tuileries, this was the first of many public monuments erected not to an individual hero but to an anonymous mass. Thorvaldsen had recourse not to allegory but to a much more abstract and conventional heraldic symbolism in which the wounded lion-couchant stands for gallantry. Also of interest is the prophetic use of a startling natural setting to add to the impact of the monument (*see* 101).

17　*Annunciation* 1842 plaster 67 × 125 cm.
　　Copenhagen, Thorvaldsens Museum
　　Thorvaldsen is generally at his most successful in relief, but one is too aware of the sculptor's stolidly logical mind to be entirely convinced. Neither angel nor Madonna quite transcend the stone from which they are cut. Here, then, is the origin of official religious sculpture of the past two hundred years.

GAETANO MONTI
b. Ravenna 1776 – d. Milan 1847

18　*The Allied Sovereigns arrive at Leipzig* 1826 bronze relief
　　Milan, Arco della Pace
　　This work is characteristic of the changes which occurred in Neo-classicism as it became increasingly a vehicle for political propaganda and documentation. Monti submerged his figures into correctly furnished space, whereas Canova used a neutral abstract ground.

JOHAN HEINRICH VON DANNECKER
Waldenbruck 1758–1841

19　*Ariadne on a panther* 1803 terracotta 29 cm.
　　Stuttgart, Staatsgalerie
　　As the Neoclassic style spread internationally it developed along the lines of Thorvaldsen's disciplined reliefs. Canova's sensuousness was slowly abandoned. But a strong Romantic undercurrent, especially in Germany, enlivened Neoclassic sculpture by its elegiac grace. Though

Dannecker held the frontal approach, the fluency of line and softness of modelling add a lyrical note, usually absent in Thorvaldsen.

JOHN FLAXMAN
b. York 1755 – d. London 1826

20　*Sketch for monument to Hon. Barbara Lowther c.* 1806 plaster 110 × 66 cm.
　　London, Victoria and Albert Museum
　　As happens with the work of many Neoclassic sculptors, Flaxman's sketches show a spontaneity which betrays their eighteenth-century origins. However pleasing this quality of improvization may be to our own tastes, it must not blind us to the fact that these sketches were considered imperfect by their creators whose true conceptions can only be gathered from their finished pieces.

21　*Monument to Lord Mansfield* 1795–1801 marble
　　London, Westminster Abbey
　　Unlike Canova, Flaxman did not invent a new type of tomb but grafted Neoclassic elements on to a traditional structure. It is primarily in the magnificently modelled head of the subject that Flaxman's real skill can be grasped. The allegories have little formal significance, inviting a guide-book reading rather than visual experience.

22　*Monument to Harriet Susan, Viscountess Fitzharris c.* 1815 marble
　　Hampshire, Christchurch Priory
　　It is in the nature of the English genius to achieve its highest fulfilment in the sensitive transcription of intimate, restrained sentiments. Tastefully economical in its reliance on realistic detail, this monument marks one of the superior moments in English sculpture.

SIR FRANCIS CHANTREY
b. Norton (Derby) 1781 – d. London 1842

23　*Mrs Jordan as Charity* 1831–4 marble 183 cm.
　　Bletchingley, Surrey, Earl of Munster Collection
　　One step beyond this charming group lies the maudlin coyness of later nineteenth-century bric-à-brac. But here we are still close enough to the unselfconscious optimism of early Romanticism, tempered by the restraint of Classicism, to avoid the pitfalls of spurious sentiment. Only the lack of compositional discipline gives a hint of what is to come.

MATTHEW COTES WYATT
London 1777–1862

24 *Monument to Princess Charlotte* 1820–4 marble
Windsor, St George's Chapel
Aspiring to the purity of Flaxman's ethereal and disembodied outline drawings, Wyatt seems to have lost sight of some of the fundamentals of sculpture. This leads him to a strange flaccidity in the figures and defeats the artist's purpose of creating light and floating forms.

PIERRE GIRAUD
b. Luc 1783 – d. Paris 1836

25 *Sketch for his wife's tomb* 1827 wax 58 × 171 cm.
Paris, Louvre
French Neoclassicism tended to be austerely dogmatic and frequently polemical, especially during the Revolutionary and Napoleonic epochs. Giraud's magnificent wax sketch is moving in its manly and sober treatment of the dead bodies. Death is suggested visually rather than dramatically by the limp arch of the bosom. The artist's attempt to preserve a native French Classicism, stemming from Poussin, is evident, though a germinal Romanticism is revealed in the very subtle movement of the figures which contrasts sharply with current Neoclassical standards. Rude (61) and also Préault (67) seem to owe much to this masterpiece.

SIR RICHARD WESTMACOTT
London 1775–1856

26 *Monument to Charles James Fox* 1810–23 marble
London, Westminster Abbey
The noble precepts of Neoclassicism can be quickly debased to cold oratory. This monument is a literary and calculated *tableau-vivant* in which the dying Fox, accompanied by a grateful Negro, is posed in stone.

JOSEPH-CHARLES MARIN
Paris 1759–1834

27 *Arcadian family c.* 1790 terracotta 55 × 51 × 23 cm.
New York, French & Company, Inc.
The boundaries between Rococo and Neoclassicism are often hard to define. Restrained surface modelling, a more static composition and broader proportions distinguish this work from Clodion's Rococo groups. The sentiment, more sober and less erotic, is symptomatic of the change.

28 *Caius Gracchus leaving his wife, Licinia* 1801 plaster bas-relief
Paris, École des Beaux-Arts
Marin's work was often in danger of becoming a compendium of ancient styles, drawing as he did on such diverse sources as the Parthenon, Hellenistic and Roman eras. Here, however, the sweeping unity of composition indicated by the large, climatic rhythms rising upward from the undulating body of Licinia through the toga folds and back again via the gesture of the bearded figure, has an unimpeachably heroic quality.

SIMON-LOUIS BOIZOT
Paris 1743–1809

29 *Apollon Musagète c.* 1786 *biscuit de Sèvres*
Sèvres, Musée Céramique
The fine-grained, dry *biscuit de Sèvres* pottery was a fine vehicle for Neo-classic expression. Unlike the lushly tinted and glazed porcelain of the Rococo, the accent is on linear silhouette rather than on fullness of volume.

ANTOINE-DENIS CHAUDET
Paris 1763–1810

30 *Amor catching a butterfly* completed posthumously (model 1802), marble 80 cm.
Paris, Louvre
Most of Chaudet's work is characterized by copybook frigidity and a total lack of invention. But the influence of contemporary French painting is seen here in the Romantic subject-matter and in the tender treatment of the flesh, both of which are reminiscent of Prud'hon.

JOSEPH CHINARD
Lyon 1756–1813

31 *Madame Récamier c.* 1802 marble 79 cm.
Lyon, Musée des Beaux-Arts
Of china-like delicacy in its finish, this bust is unquestionably one of the most piquant and attractive sculptures in the modern French

32

33

34

35

37

38

36

39

repertory. The frontal bust, nonchalantly draped and surmounted by a sly, sideward glancing head, gives an effect of great intimacy.

ANTONIO CANOVA (*see* 2)

32 *Madame Récamier* 1813 marble 46 × 29 × 19 cm.
Passagno, Gipsoteca Canoviana
The intelligent, nevertheless playful woman, rather than the slightly perverse girl, is the subject of Canova's portrait. Though piously rapt, an ironic smile betrays an enchanting reality beneath the equally enchanting mask.

JOSEPH CHINARO (*see* 31)

33 *Apollo crushing Superstition underfoot* 1791 terracotta 51 cm.
Paris, Musée Carnavalet
The turbulent life of this artist who repeatedly risked his head during the Revolution is not reflected in his work. It is astonishing to see how fluently Chinard manages to hide the discrepancy between Revolutionary content, implied by the militant subject of secularization, and a hyper-refined Classic style. The peculiar mixture of eroticism and moral 'message' is prophetic of the *fin de siècle*, especially Moreau (145).

GOTTFRIED SCHADOW

Berlin 1764–1850

34 *Monument to Princess Louise and Princess Friederike of Mecklenburg-Schwerin* 1795 plaster 172 cm.
Berlin, Staatliche Museen
German Neoclassicism is marked by an overt strain of Romantic sentiment. *Schwärmerei*, that concept of tenderness, yearning, devotion and high moral worth, finds its most charming embodiment in Schadow's portrait of these two royal sisters. One became Queen of Prussia (36).

35 *Tomb of Graf Alexander von der Mark* 1787–91 marble 6 m.
Berlin, Dorotheenstädtische Kirche
Schadow bases himself directly on a Roman tomb in the Lateran. The suggestion of the boy's having fallen asleep while playing is rendered more poignant by being contrasted to the relief of the Three Fates. The upper figures, harsh in theme and cramped in composition give the fully modelled body of the child a softer vulnerability.

CHRISTIAN-DANIEL RAUCH

b. Arolsen (Germany) 1777 – d. Dresden 1857

36 *Tomb of Queen Louise c.* 1815 marble 87 × 233 × 90 cm. (figure): 80 × 269 × 124 cm. (base)
Berlin, Charlottenburg Mausoleum
The theatricality of the setting with its blue-glass windows giving the funerary image a spectral aura, brings us to the point at which Neoclassicism turned to admittedly Romantic effect despite Classical ornamental trappings.

ASMUS-JAKOB CARSTENS

b. St Jurgensby (Denmark) 1754 – d. Rome 1798

37 *One of the Fates* 1794 plaster 48 cm.
Frankfurt a. M., Städelsches Kunstinstitut
This sculpture is Classic in formal conception but charged with a brooding emotional impact. The artist's interest in the more mysterious areas of Greek mythology, instead of the usual Olympian subjects, can be interpreted simultaneously as either Romantic or Neoclassic.

JOHAN TOBIAS SERGEL

Stockholm 1740–1814

38 *Mars and Venus* 1771–2 terracotta 41 cm.
Gothenburg, Konstmuseum
Northern artists often infused a dramatic momentum into their sculpture inconsistent with their Classical subjects and ostensibly Classical style. Here violently colliding spiral and diagonal masses are held together by a remarkably firm silhouette.

JOHAN-NIKLAS BYSTRÖM

b. Filipstad (Sweden) 1783 – d. Rome 1848

39 *Juno and the infant Hercules (origin of the Milky Way) c.* 1828 marble 202 × 86 cm.
Stockholm, Nationalmuseum
Neoclassic artists did not restrict themselves to the Greco-Roman repertory but also copied works of the High Renaissance. For this sculpture Giorgione's *Sleeping Venus* served as inspiration. In the process of translation, however, the candid sensuousness of Giorgione's has been eliminated in favour of a glassy smoothness of surface and form.

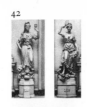

40

42

41

43

44

45

46

47

48

JOHN GIBSON
b. Gyffin (Wales) 1791 – d. Rome 1866

40 *Hylas and the water-nymphs* 1826 198 cm.
London, Tate Gallery
Gibson studied under Canova and Thorvaldsen, and accepted from them the rigorous tenets of Neoclassicism. In this interpretation of Hylas about to be drowned by the caress of enamoured water-nymphs, he disposes his figures as if they were seen in relief, reduces gestures to a minimum.

HIRAM POWERS
b. Woodstock, Vermont, U.S.A., 1805 – d. Florence 1873

41 *The Greek slave* 1846 marble 157 cm.
Washington, D.C., Corcoran Gallery of Art
The most celebrated American sculpture of the nineteenth century was exhibited with great success in London and Paris, giving rise to new critical attitudes towards American art, both at home and abroad. Powers's concern for a very delicate transcription of the human form animated by a tender silhouette is already remarkably close to the compact serenity of Maillol (170).

WILLIAM RUSH
Philadelphia 1756–1833

42 *Comedy and Tragedy* 1808 painted pine: *Comedy* 269 cm. *Tragedy* 255 cm.
Philadelphia, Pa, Pennsylvania Academy of the Fine Arts
Very little monumental sculpture was produced in America during the first half of the nineteenth century. Rush's attitude in this group is forthright and provincial, and he is saved from pomposity by his very limitations. Important for future American sculpture is the heterodox attitude towards materials. Instead of using bronze and marble, American sculptors have frequently turned to heavily grained or even polychromed wood and forged iron.

VALENTIN SONNENSCHEIN
b. Stuttgart 1749 – d. Berne 1828

43 *Portrait of a Berne alderman c.* 1780–90 terracotta 29 cm.
Berne, Kunstmuseum
Sonnenschein was primarily a porcelain designer and his independent sculptures retain the fetchingly diminutive grace of his trade. His sharp

observation and high regard for realism distinguish him from his stylistically more sophisticated French colleagues.

BARTOLOMEO PINELLI
Rome 1781–1835

44 *The wounded brigand c.* 1830 terracotta 37 cm.
Rome, Museo di Roma
Pinelli, whose father was a carver of figurines, retains all the realism and earthiness of that trade. He reconciled his talent for observation with his Neoclassic ambitions by insisting that modern Rome was an extension of its ancient self. Thus he hoped that a realistic transcription of his native surroundings would lead him to the purest form of Classicism.

LORENZO BARTOLINI
b. Vernio (Tuscany) 1777 – d. Florence 1850

45 *Trust in God* 1835 marble 95 × 60 cm.
& Milan, Museo Poldi-Pezzoli
46 A cherished friend of Ingres, Bartolini is a close sculptural parallel to the great French painter. The fine balance between minute description of flesh and a purely cerebral elaboration of abstract line, between fullness of modelling and astringent control over each volume make the rear view of this figure closely related to *Le bain turc*.

47 *The wine-presser c.* 1842–4 (original *c.* 1818) marble 135 cm.
Florence, Marchese Bufalini Collection
Bartolini created a considerable stir by drawing his inspiration from Quattrocento (i.e. non-Classical) painting. His choice of Benozzo Gozzoli was deliberate and indicated his sympathy with fresh, naturalistic narrative to the detriment of Classical dogma. He also became one of the first artists to open nineteenth-century eyes to the values of Quattrocento art.

48 *Monument to Princess Czartoryski of Warsaw* 1837–44 marble 187 cm.
& Florence, Sta Croce
49 This monument was commissioned for the most important funerary church in Florence and Bartolini had to compete with a great number of notable Quattrocento tombs. Basing his work on earlier examples, he produced a tomb which is as expressive of nineteenth-century

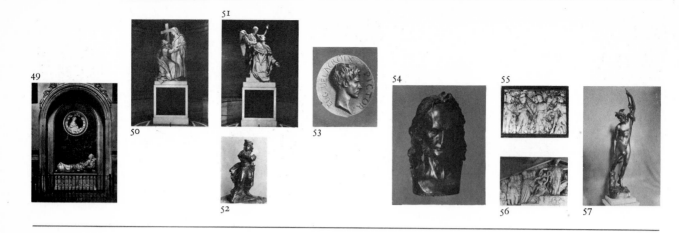

attitudes towards religion and death and has nothing in common with
the far more transcendental treatment displayed in Quattrocento works
of the same nature. Even the Madonna, isolated from the corpse by a
dark marble wall, becomes a picture on a wall rather than an immanent
presence blessing the dead. The intensity of religious devotion may be
unchanged but the relationship between God and man has become far
more complex, requiring an intricate, oblique expression.

JEAN-PIERRE CORTOT
Paris, 1787–1843

50 *Marie-Antoinette succoured by religion c.* 1827 marble 225 cm.
Paris, Chapelle Expiatoire
This, and the following group, were commissioned during the Restoration as an act of public atonement for the regicide committed by
Revolutionary tribunals. Typical of what will later in this text be called
Academic art is the unresolved cheek-by-jowl relationship of dryly
accurate, documentary realism, the photographic likeness of the queen
and her cloak, and the abstractly Classical, impersonal and utterly stony
allegorical figure which is meant to give historical events greater dignity
and meaning.

FRANÇOIS-JOSEPH BOSIO
b. Monaco 1768 – d. Paris 1855

51 *Apotheosis of Louis XVI* 1825 marble 225 cm.
Paris, Chapelle Expiatoire
The anonymity of official Classicism under the Restoration becomes
painfully evident when this sculpture is compared with the preceding
plate. Technically of great efficiency and fairly well endowed with a
certain talent for theatrical effect, Bosio seems to be directing a rehearsal
of a play rather than the actual representation. The actors are neither
convinced nor convincing.

DAVID D'ANGERS
b. Angers 1788 – d. Paris 1856

52 *Le Grand Condé* 1817 bronze 37 cm.
Paris, Louvre
David d'Angers was perhaps the most typical of Romantic sculptors,
having been nursed in the turmoil of the Revolution and coming to
maturity during the heroic years of the Napoleonic epoch. His most

renowned work, this impetuous image of Condé inciting his soldiers to
follow him in the attack, expresses all the fiery disregard for Classical
convention inherent in Romanticism.

53 *Medal with profile of Delacroix* 1828 bronze 10 cm. diameter
Angers, Musée des Beaux-Arts
Unlike the Classicists whose heroes are distinguished by their virtuous
dignity, the Romantics worship the passionate rebel. No other likeness
of Delacroix achieves the finesse of this model. The painter's high-bred
sensibility is expressed by swift light-dark modelling and by a flashing
silhouette that is both taut and flexible.

54 *Nicolò Paganini* 1830 bronze 62 × 38 × 34 cm.
Angers, Musée des Beaux-Arts
It was the declared aim of David d'Angers to control his highly
personal interpretations of character by means of phrenological
measurements. He tried to follow Lavater, the German poet and
physiognomist, in attributing definite temperamental significance to
various cranial forms.

55 *Battle of Fleurus. General Jourdan refuses to accept his enemy's sword* 1835
plaster bas-relief 110 × 156 cm.
Angers, Musée des Beaux-Arts
Swift and deft touches of summary but convincing modelling give a
sense of 'handwriting' to the sketches of David d'Angers, adding to
their pleasing *élan*. But even among Romantic sculptors the rupture
between figure and environment, first described by Neoclassic artists,
was not healed. For a new vision which grasps both figure and the
matrix of the figure, we have to wait for the mature works of Rodin
(127).

56 *Pediment of the Panthéon* 1837 plaster bas-relief 290 cm.
Angers, Musée des Beaux-Arts
Daring and wilfully insistent on the necessity of finding his own
sculptural principles when creating 'private' sculpture, David d'Angers,
along with his Romantic colleagues, became docile in his recourse to
Classical conventions when given a public commission. Although
certain details show the artist's habitual *brio*, the overall effect is
unconvincing and graceless.

FRANÇOIS RUDE
b. Dijon 1789 – d. Paris 1855

57 *Mercury* 1834 bronze 250 cm.
Paris, Louvre
The dependence on previous styles introduced into modern sculpture by Neoclassicism was continued in early works by the greatest exponent of Romanticism in sculpture. In this, Rude's first public success, he blended the sleek elegance of Pigalle with the nervous strain of Giambologna. The eclecticism of Rude's early style, though strong, is nevertheless outweighed by that spontaneous command over plastic rhythms and intuitive feeling for logical counterpoise of volumes characteristic of all born sculptors.

58 *Neapolitan fisherboy with tortoise* 1833 marble 77 × 47 cm.
Paris, Louvre
For decades Naples was the goal and inspiration of artists. First prized for its antiquities, then beloved for the colourful 'romantic' ways of its vagabonds, it was a Mecca also because of its virtuoso Baroque sculptures. All these elements of Classical innocence, Romantic exoticism and realistic execution can be found in this most charming of Rude's smaller figures (*see* II).

59 *Marshal Ney* 1852–3 bronze 266 cm.
Paris, Avenue de l'Observatoire
The Napoleonic epic, prime sustenance for French Romanticism, finds its greatest interpreter in Rude. The impassioned figure of Marshal Ney leading his men into battle displays an exquisite balance between an action glorified by being part of the legendary past and the sense of excitement at reliving the past action in the present. As in most of Rude's successful work, the composition is extravagantly dynamic and yet extremely clear in its complex elaboration.

60 *La Marseillaise* (*song of the departing volunteers*) 1833–6 stone 127 × 6 m.
Paris, Arc de Triomphe
In an age when the theatre spoke to a nationwide audience more successfully than any other art, it is hardly surprising to find sculpture becoming more and more theatrical. Rarely, however, has histrionic gesture been so persuasively reconciled with sculpturally organic form as here.

61 *Tomb of Godefroi de Cavaignac* 1845–7 bronze 200 cm.
Paris, Cimetière de Montmartre
The almost clinical depiction of a corpse blends involuntarily with associations of late-Gothic tomb sculpture. Rarely has the exhaustion of death been so successfully conveyed. Each detail, such as the eerily graceful hand stretched beyond the subtly spiralling shroud, relates itself to the whole with the unforced logic of all natural things. No allegories, no mourners are allowed to interfere with this image of death, and it is this singleness of purpose, the heroic economy of the artist, which gives death its overwhelming finality.

62 *Napoleon awakening to immortality* 1845 plaster 215 × 195 cm.
Paris, Louvre
Commissioned by an admirer of Napoleon for a private park, this sculpture is perhaps the most important point of departure for Rodin (114 on). The free mixing of relief and sculpture-in-the-round, the heaving rhythm of the surfaces and the sense of form emerging from amorphous mass, all this must have been an inspiration to Rodin, who may also have had this particular piece of sculpture in mind when he decided to shroud his *Balzac* in a dressing-gown (130).

63 ANTOINE-AUGUSTIN PRÉAULT
& Paris 1810–79
64 *Christ on the Cross* 1840 wood 260 cm.
Paris, Église St Gervais-et-St Protais
Romanticism was expressed in emotional subjects emotionally interpreted, but it was also the result of a strong desire to find ties with basic realities after the speculative abstractions of late-Neoclassic art. A feeling of kinship with workers and peasants who led a simple life close to earthy realities made itself felt as well as the urge to reinterpret religious sentiment.

Powerfully modelled, both realistic and exalted, this crucifix with its deliberate choice of an 'ignoble' material and its consequent association with peasant carvings is the most successful of modern religious sculptures. Place close to the ground by the artist, a method which was later adopted by Rodin, in order to break down the artificial frontiers between art and life, its expression of anguish is startlingly direct and physical.

65 *Massacre* 1834 bronze 108 × 138 cm.
Chartres, Musée des Beaux-Arts
This sculpture was the nineteenth-century prototype for future developments. Not only its violent and irrational subject but the violent and
irrational mode of representation (it is impossible to determine the
continuity of forms or their spatial relationships) and the fact that, for
the first time, a fragment was conceived as a finished work made this
sculpture truly epochal. Many critics have suggested that it is intimately
linked with the creation of Picasso's *Guernica*.

FÉLICIE DE FAUVEAU
Florence 1799–1886
66 *Tomb of the sculptress's mother* 1858 marble
Florence, Carmine
Little is left of the work of one of the most influential and flamboyant
personalities of the Romantic era. Even her most famous work, a
monument to Dante of which she had completed several fragments,
has disappeared. In her Florentine *salon*, Félicie de Fauveau preached the
beauties of Trecento and Quattrocento art to the intellectual *élite* of
Europe. Her work mirrors these interests. Realistic elements are linked
with highly stylized Quattrocento borrowings. She herself was conscious of this eclecticism and justified it by proclaiming that the artist
should have complete freedom of choice stylistically and thematically.

ANTOINE-AUGUSTIN PRÉAULT (*see* 63)
67 *Ophelia* 1876 bronze (original 1843) 61 × 201 cm.
Marseilles, Musée de Longchamps
Among Préault's last works is this astonishingly modern Ophelia which
not only presages the wafting forms of Art Nouveau but also represents
an important step in that peculiarly modern trend which tries to present
the figure in its environment. Ophelia's body as it trails in the water
becomes one with it like a water plant. The Shakespearean subject and
resemblance to French tomb effigies are typical of Romanticism.

ALEXANDER MUNRO
b. Inverness 1825 – d. Cannes 1871
68 *Paolo and Francesca* 1852 marble 66 × 65 × 54 cm.
Birmingham, City Museum and Art Gallery
The only sculptor who, though not a member, was a guiding spirit of
the Pre-Raphaelites, Munro had a preciousness and morbidity which
related him to his painter friends. Unlike Pre-Raphaelite painters,
however, Munro preserved an economy of detail which was astonishingly forward-looking, and allowed great concentration on the
emotional impact of his figures.

THÉODORE GÉRICAULT
b. Rouen 1791 – d. Paris 1824
69 *Nymph and satyr* 1817–20 terracotta 16 cm.
Buffalo, N.Y., Albright-Knox Gallery, George B. and Jennie R.
Matthews Fund
This composition can be compared with Canova's *Cupid and Psyche* (4).
Although both compositions centre round a circular void, the earlier
piece is restrained by line whereas the later one is constantly impelled
by explosive mass. It represents the full progress of Romanticism:
struggle, passionate violence, centrifugal motion and the eloquent
evidence of the artist's intervention in the rough surface handling.

ANTOINE-LOUIS BARYE
Paris 1796–1875
70 *Theseus and the Minotaur* 1849–52 bronze 43 cm.
Paris, Louvre
Even when dealing with a Classical theme, Barye insists on a trenchant,
novel solution. By going back to the elemental, sacred ritual of the
Greek *agon*, Barye finds a forceful meaning in the struggle as well as
a tense resolution of vectors which serves as a link between Greek
Archaic sculpture and Bourdelle (171 on), at once hieratic and intensely
alive.

71 *Fortitude protecting Labour* 1859 plaster 25 cm.
Paris, Louvre
One of the few public commissions accorded the greatest sculptor of
his time increases our sense of loss: what might Barye not have done if
he had found the necessary financial support? Grandiose without grandi-
loquence, vibrant in its surface effects, superbly proportioned to suit the
monumental scale, this is one of the few dignified public monuments of
the nineteenth century. So well does the sculpture insert itself into the
court façade of the Louvre that few visitors, as they enter the museum
portals, are aware of passing under one of Barye's masterpieces.

72

74

75

76

78

79

73

77

72 *Bull attacked by a tiger* exhibited posthumously, bronze 19 × 22 cm.
Paris, Louvre
The dynamic treatment of surface and rhythmic relationship between volumes served to inspire Rodin at a later date and led to the concept of the autonomy of sculpture as an organism in its own right. Here the base has shrivelled and the sculpture juts out beyond its limits, thus piercing the ambience of the animal and impinging on our own world.

73 *Jaguar devouring a hare* 1852 bronze 42 × 93 cm.
Paris, Louvre
Romantic themes of death, bloodlust and savage instincts were treated by Barye with a sensitive regard for both artistic demands and zoologically correct realism. The result is one of the most convincing statements about the nature of animal existence in the history of sculpture. His development of forms swelling under the surface and the awareness of surface as a ligament instead of a merely decorative plane were of great importance to later sculptors (*see* 182).

74 *Napoleon on horseback* 1856 bronze 135 cm.
Paris, Louvre
Only this sensitive bronze *bozzetto* is left of a monumental project which envisaged four equestrians disposed on a lozenge-shaped piazza against the backdrop of Corsican mountains. The interplay between immobile weight (rider) and the resilient, flexing support (horse) is of an originality comparable with the equestrians of the Quattrocento.

75 *Young nude woman* 1846 plaster and wax 21 cm.
Paris, Louvre
Along with Préault, Barye is among the precursors of Rodin in discovering the fragment as a device for the expression of contemporary conditions. But, whereas Préault's and Rodin's conceptions of the torso are tragic, Barye's sculpture has a radiant clarity, a triumphant rejection of the divorce of mind and matter.

JEAN-JACQUES PRADIER
b. Geneva 1792 – d. Rueil (France) 1852

76 *Laundress c.* 1850 plaster 34 × 14 cm.
Geneva, Musée d'Art et d'Histoire
'The wretched state of modern sculpture', wrote Baudelaire in his *Salon of 1846* 'is proved by Pradier being its king.' However, this older sister of Zola's Gervaise and Degas's laundresses is a piquant combination of social document and erotic trifle of great competence and engaging wit. It is also one of the first signs of a Rococo revival in sculpture.

JEAN-BAPTISTE CLÉSINGER
b. Besançon 1814 – d. 1883

77 *Woman bitten by a serpent* 1847 marble 58 × 178 cm.
Paris, Louvre
Though extravagantly praised by Baudelaire, whose poetic image of womankind seems to be illustrated here (the model was Apollonice Sabatier, Baudelaire's mistress) Clésinger's masterpiece is obscured for our eyes by too many imitations which bowdlerized an originally erotic theme. The sinuous counter-motions of nude and snake, the dream-like air demand admiration, while the composition presaging both Art Nouveau and Munch, the Norwegian Expressionist painter, is historically important.

HONORÉ DAUMIER
b. Marseilles 1808 – d. Valmondois 1879

78 *The burden c.* 1855 terracotta 35 cm.
Paris, Paul Rosenberg Collection
A close observer of the proletarian life of Paris, Daumier is perhaps the only sculptor who takes up social themes without being either mawkish or conventional. Inspired by the spiralling force of certain Michelangelo figures, Daumier elevates and dignifies to a humble theme without losing sight of the daily unheroic fatigue suffered by his protagonists. This work may have served as a preparatory study for Daumier's painting *La Lavandeuse*.

JEAN-PIERRE DANTAN
b. Paris 1800 – d. Bade 1869

79 *Balzac* 1835 plaster 34 cm.
Paris, Musée Carnavalet
The Romantic sardonic humour is here translated into sculpture. Dantan created hundreds of caricatures of Parisian characters which were exhibited with great success. Though they are often charming, their effect derives neither from a true gift for penetrating psychological

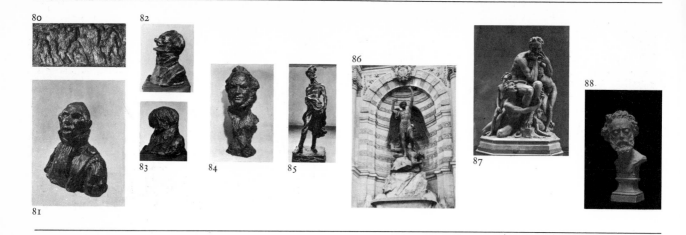

judgement nor from a grasp of sculptural form, but rather from a more commonplace and mechanical distortion of salient features (*see* 81–3).

HONORÉ DAUMIER (*see* 78)

80 *Migrants c.* 1870 bronze 28 × 66 cm.
Paris, Geoffrey-Déchaume Collection
Compared with the later attempts of Dalou (106) to represent the sufferings of the proletariat, Daumier's interpretations always retain an epic force which avoids sentimentality. Instead of individual migrant workers, Daumier here represents a nation on the march. The format suggests a continuous frieze evoking the impulse of the procession, but the accents and intervals are so beautifully placed that the relief has a compact, static structure as well.

81 *The orator: bust of André Dupin at the French Parliament c.* 1832 bronze
15 cm.
Marseille, Musée des Beaux-Arts
Even though Daumier's characters are not involved in a dramatic situation, we can judge how they would react under any given circumstances. Sly, servile, treacherous, dissolute – the most subtle and conflicting gradations of temperament are expressed by a quickly changing, utterly convincing variety of volumes and voids.

82 *Toothless laughter c.* 1832 bronze 16 cm.
Marseille, Musée des Beaux-Arts
By suppressing those parts of a physiognomy which are psychologically meaningless, Daumier achieves a forceful nakedness of characterization in which only the most generalized characteristics of expression are allowed to exist. Thus he gives us the eternal essentials of even the most foolishly ephemeral of mortals.

83 *Prunelle c.* 1830–2 bronze 13 cm.
Marseille, Musée des Beaux-Arts
Daumier was alone in having the gift of finding a formal solution which did justice both to the demands of his subject and the sculptural exigencies of his material. Dissatisfied with merely humorous realism, he invented a language of discontinuous form which gave his heads the effect of being modelled from the inside out as if from pressure beneath the skin.

84 *Self-portrait c.* 1855 bronze 72 cm.
Paris, Bibliothèque Nationale
Self-portraits in sculpture were rare before Canova and the relatively large number we have in the nineteenth century suggests the greater degree of selfconsciousness imposed by Romanticism. Involuntarily Daumier presents himself a little like his admired Rembrandt, with his near-sighted eyes straining for clearer vision.

85 *Ratapoil* 1850 bronze 38 cm.
Paris, Louvre
Ratapoil was Daumier's most ambitious creation. It preserves the free modelling of his spontaneous on-the-spot caricatures but goes beyond these minor works in its monumental sense of scale and structure. Rodin (*see* 114–on) owes a good deal to the exquisite nobility of form and surface, the space-embracing fling of the limbs and the irresistibly expressive pose of *Ratapoil*. This figure became a public symbol, castigating the bankrupt swagger of the Second Empire.

FRANCISQUE-JOSEPH DURET
Paris 1804–65
86 *St Michael overcoming the Devil* 1860–1 bronze 5·5 m.
Paris, Place Saint-Michel
A competent sculptor best known for having been Carpeaux's teacher, Duret was at his best when faced with monumental commissions which demanded intelligent rather brilliant solutions. His task here was to give shape and focus to an amorphous clearing in the tangle of the modern metropolis and to harmonize an architecturally discordant scene by means of sculpture.

JEAN-BAPTISTE CARPEAUX
b. Valenciennes 1827 – d. Courbevoie 1875
87 *Ugolino and his children* 1860–2 marble 200 m.
Valenciennes, Musée des Beaux-Arts
Executed and exhibited at Rome while Carpeaux was at the Académie, *Ugolino* was very well received because of its impeccable yet impetuous modelling. The composition has a massiveness which gives great weight to the pathos of the central figure. When exhibited later in Paris, however, the group was much criticized by the Academicians.

89 90 91 92 93 94 95 96

88 *Bruno Chérier* 1875 plaster 62 cm.
Paris, Louvre
Whereas most of Carpeaux's official portraits are appealing on account of their exquisite lightness and *brio*, his more personal portraits of friends reveal a depth of penetration and honesty of emotional response that rank them with the greatest portraits of the past. Though his virtuosity in handling is brilliant, his execution is always yoked to an intense search for an appropriately expressive form.

89 *Mademoiselle Fiocre* 1869 plaster 82 cm.
Paris, Louvre
Just as *Ugolino* inspired Rodin to greater emotional expression (in *The thinker*), so Carpeaux's portraits in their vivacity and fresh appreciation of character became important for Rodin's early portraits. Going back to eighteenth-century portraits such as those by Houdon, Carpeaux was perhaps the only artist of his century who could celebrate sheer fashionable physical loveliness without becoming banal.

90 *Flora* 1866 terracotta 290 × 360 cm.
Paris, Louvre
Breaking through the barriers set by Academic traditions, Carpeaux mingled relief freely with cutting in the round, again opening the way for future developments. The brilliant interplay of light and dark is used with especial advantage in the central figure, giving it an aura of subdued and suffused light against which the vigorously sensuous forms develop towards their characteristic ripeness.

91 *Fontaine de l'Observatoire: the four quarters of the globe* 1868–9 bronze 220 cm.
Paris, Jardin du Luxembourg
Effortlessly, these four allegorical figures support the globe, their ripe and sinuous bodies stretching and reaching with motions that are consummately robust and graceful. Most amazing of all is the ease with which the span between the figures is bridged by an intricate, yet never laboriously studied congruence of rhythms which also serve to define the space dividing one from the other.

92 *The dance* 1868–9 stone
Paris, façade of the Opéra

His greatest sculpture caused Carpeaux the greatest grief because of its adverse reception. Nowhere else has he expressed himself so fully as *boulevardier*, as intelligent artist and as the last pagan spirit surviving into a modern age. The verve of the figures, their free development in space are of a mastery which defies competition.

ADRIANO CECIONI
b. Fontebuona (Italy) 1838 – d. Florence 1886
93 *Cocotte* 1875 terracotta 48 cm.
Milan, J. Gabriolo Collection
Keen observation and a light hand in giving sculptural substance to a casual stance of finely shaded impudence keep this figure from sinking to the level of a 'conversation piece'. Cecioni was regarded with suspicion by officialdom but became an inspiration for later generations of Italian artists.

GIOVANNI DUPRÉ
b. Siena 1817 – d. 1882
94 *Abel* 1842 bronze 228 × 72 cm.
Florence, Galleria d'Arte Moderna
So shockingly lively did this statue seem when it was first exhibited that the young artist was accused of having made a plaster case of his subject. Indeed, the freedom of modelling and the steadfast investigation of reality are prophetic of Rodin's *The Age of Bronze* (116) which was criticized on the same grounds. It is curious to follow these allegations of too great a naturalism down to its ultimate conclusion in our own day (345).

ACHILLE D'ORSI
95 Naples 1845–1929
& *Fantasy – Sleep* terracotta 28 × 24 cm.
96 Fiesole, Villa Dupré
Not infrequently provincial artists, left to their own devices by lack of public and critical attention, produce works of forward-looking boldness which surpass the work of more sophisticated colleagues. The extraordinary disorientation of scale, the haunting interpretations and the unexpected composition of this piece expanded the horizons of nineteenth-century sculptural possibilities.

317

97 98 99 100 101 102 103

PIETRO MAGNI
b. 1817 – d. Milan 1877

97 *Monument to commemorate the cutting of the Suez Canal* 1858–63 marble, base 103 × 162 × 162 cm., group 190 × 143 × 143 cm.
Trieste, Civico Museo Revoltella

The tenacity with which the nineteenth century insisted on investing hard economic and technical events with allegorical nobility gives this sculpture a specially touching appeal. The completion of the Suez Canal is celebrated by genteel nymphs and gods . . . and incidentally by the first performance of *Aïda*.

ALBERT-ERNEST CARRIER-BELLEUSE
b. Anizy-le-Château 1824 – d. Sèvres 1887

98 *Triton carrying a nymph c.* 1860 terracotta 64 cm.
London, David Barclay Ltd

Today's partiality for audacious styles has relegated Carrier-Belleuse, Rodin's greatest rival, to oblivion. It is true that he is not powerfully inventive. He belongs rather to that class of artists whose strength lies in carrying already established principles to a new peak of elegant perfection.

ALFRED STEVENS
b. Blandford (Dorset) 1817 – d. London 1875

99 *Monument to the Duke of Wellington* erected 1875 marble and bronze
London, St Paul's Cathedral

The *malaise* of monumental sculpture which grew acute in the latter half of the nineteenth century makes itself felt here in exaggerations, and in the double source of inspiration: French sixteenth-century tombs and Florentine fifteenth-century equestrian statues. The main burden of extolling the glory of Wellington is borne by architecture rather than by sculptural elements.

CARLO MAROCHETTI
b. Turin 1805 – d. Paris 1867

100 *Monument to Emanuele Filiberto* 1838 bronze
Turin, Piazza San Carlo

Marochetti's most successful sculpture derives its strength not only from the liveliness of horse and rider but from the very cleverly adjusted relationship of format between pedestal and the eighteenth-century

square surrounding it. Yet the peculiar lack of continuity between the serene harmonies of eighteenth-century architecture and nineteenth-century posturing persists – and probably inspired de Chirico's piazza paintings (*see* p. 38).

FRÉDÉRIC-AUGUSTE BARTHOLDI
b. Colmar 1834 – d. Paris 1904

101 *The Lion of Belfort* 1875–80 red sandstone 11 × 22 m.
Belfort, Château

Basing his design on Thorvaldsen's *Lion of Lucerne* (16), Bartholdi depends on sheer size for the impact and originality of his monument. What he has failed to achieve in sculptural terms, the artist has made good in his extremely intelligent choice of location affording a majestic span of space between town and monument (*see* p. 35).

102 *The Statue of Liberty* constructed 1875–84, erected 1886; hammered
&
103 copper sheets; stone pedestal; statue 46·43 m. to top of torch; pedestal 25·7 m., base 20·24 m.; entire statue over 91·44 m.
New York Harbour

Two important themes, the emigration of vast masses in search of liberty and work, and the rise of American power, are interpreted in terms of traditional and irrelevant allegory. The immensity of the project, however, required the collaboration of the engineer, Eiffel; and his armature in its flexible, airy grace is more sculpturally valid, more expressive of an industrial age than the finished statue.

AIMÉ-JULES DALOU
Paris 1838–1902

104 *Triomphe de la République* 1899 bronze 12·13 × 22·00 × 8 m.
&
105 Paris, Place de la Nation

Returning from political exile, Dalou was commissioned to commemorate the rebirth of the Republic. In execution and composition, this monument bears comparison with the best nineteenth-century sculpture, but Dalou, dealing with an abstract anonymous concept, was incapable of inventing a new formal language which might express his idea. His is a monument to liberalism couched in reactionary terms.

106 *Sketch for the monument to Labour* 1889–91 plaster 10 cm.
London, Bourdon House

104

105

106

107

108

109

110

111

112

113

The individual figures are modelled with remarkable vigour combined with monumental disdain for extraneous detail and irrelevant oratory. Yet the proletarian ideal which was his subject did not allow of individualization, and the monument was ultimately doomed to failure because realistical figural sculpture remains essentially illustrative and therefore miniaturist in character.

107   *Head of sleeping baby* 1878 terracotta 31 × 18 × 18 cm.
Paris, Musée du Petit Palais
Illustrating the torment of an oppressive dream, this bust shows an unexpected affinity with Brancusi's early interpretation of the same theme (186). Unconventional in his finish and in his sense of the fragmentary, Dalou, though never as influential as Rodin, nevertheless rivals the great master in his honest and direct rendering of reality, and in the deep sympathy with which he apprehends all things.

108   *Woman taking off her stockings c.* 1870–80 plaster 21 cm.
London, Tate Gallery, gift of Mrs Charles Gordon
Dalou's powerful sense of realism, though it failed him when working on monumental projects, comes to his rescue in more intimate sculptures such as this. A refined and devoted sense of observation, the ability to perceive and project the intimacy of casual moments give his works a warmth which is equalled by his great compositional skill, and forecasts the work of Degas (133 on).

Designed by M. Panissera b. Turin 1830 – d. Rome 1885, model by Luigi Belli, Turin 1848–1919. Executed by students of the Royal Academy, Turin

109   *Monument to the completion of the Fréjus Tunnel* 1879
Turin, Piazza dello Statuto
How little Vela was understood by his own contemporaries can be gauged by comparing his Tunnel monument (112) with this monument on an identical theme. Rather than take the trouble to understand the character and the ethos of the modern labourer, the artists have used a time-worn allegory, akin to the 'Fall of the Titans', together with an incongruous realism.

CONSTANTIN MEUNIER
b. Etterbeek 1831 – d. Ixelles 1905

110   *The stevedore* 1903
Antwerp, Suikerrui
Meunier did in sculpture for the urban proletariat what Zola had done for it in literature. Meunier may not have encompassed all the inherent possibilities of his theme, but at least he gave to proletarian society an archetype which was to be as commonly accepted and recognized as Van Dyck's characterization of the English gentleman was in the seventeenth century.

111   *Fire-damp* 1903 bronze 120 cm.
Brussels, Musée Constantin Meunier
Translating the theme of the Pietà into modern terms, Meunier has achieved one of the most overwhelming sculptural statements of industrial tragedy. Anonymous as a medieval *gisant* (teeth clenched, the neck straining for breath), the brutally destroyed figure of a dead miner lies prostrate at the feet of a brooding woman.

VINCENZO VELA
Ligornetto (Switzerland) 1820–91

112   *Victims of labour: monument in honour of the workers who died during the building of the St Gotthard Tunnel c.* 1882 224 × 327 cm.
Ligornetto, Museo Vela
Most of the projected monuments to the decisive factors of modern life, the proletariat and mechanization, remained incomplete. Inspired, as was his contemporary Strindberg, the playwright, by the opening of the St Gotthard Tunnel as a symbol of progress and fraternity, Vela's monumental relief suggests the darkness of the tunnel and the mute, manly encounter.

113   *Tomb of Contessa d'Adda* 1849 plaster 371 cm. (base 225 × 130 cm.)
Ligornetto, Museo Vela
A new sobriety closes the series of great nineteenth-century tombs. The nobility of Bartolini's evocation (48) of past ideals is rejected. The human being vanishes into her surroundings, and the valance of a canopy demands as much attention as the head of the defunct. By a miracle of discreet staging, Vela has rescued the hands and face of the Contessa before they disappear for ever into the welter of irrelevant objects which surround and often dominate human life.

319

AUGUSTE RODIN
b. Paris 1840 – d. Meudon 1917

114 *Mask of man with a broken nose* 1864 bronze 24 × 22 × 27 cm.
Paris, Musée Rodin
In his first completely characteristic work, Rodin swept into the past
all the official principles of sculpture. Realistic in his choice of theme,
expending all his virtuosity on the clay in order to make it take on a life
of quickened light and shade, Rodin produced a sculpture which created
a scandal. The scandal, however, was salutary. Because of it, sculpture
became a living issue for almost the whole nation.

115 *Head of Rose Beuret* 1876 plaster 40 cm.
Paris, Musée Rodin
The fluency with which Rodin controlled his modelling, the variety of
style and the ease with which he sculpturally grasped almost any theme
can be seen in a comparison between this head, lyrically intimate,
strongly characterized, which is all nuance and caress, and the *Mask of
man with a broken nose*, aggressive in style and titanically handled.

116 *The Age of Bronze* 1876 bronze 180 cm.
Minneapolis Institute of Arts
This sculpture struck Rodin's contemporaries as so nakedly real that he
was accused of taking casts from nature. With the wisdom of hindsight,
we can easily distinguish the distortions, which exclude any thought of
casting from life. But the forcefulness, the inextinguishable vitality
remains and explains why Rodin's audience, faced with such a charge of
élan vital recoiled, thinking that it had gazed on life itself instead of on
sculpture (*see* 94).

117 *St John the Baptist preaching* 1878 bronze 200 cm.
New York, Museum of Modern Art
Boldly striding through the land impelled by his apostolic prophecy,
this St John is of the race of Préault's *Christ* (63). For the first time in
the nineteenth century a sculpture of monumental proportions was
brought directly into contact with daily life. The negligible base is
overshadowed by a gesture which gives St John's sermon an overwhelming directness.

118 *The old courtesan (la belle qui fut la heaulmière)* c. 1885 bronze 50 × 25
& × 30 cm.
119 118 New York, Metropolitan Museum of Art, gift of Thomas F. Ryan,
1910
119 Paris, Musée Rodin
Among Rodin's most potent gifts was his talent for compressing the
biography of an individual as well as the *condition humaine* into single
figures. The corruption of the flesh, the passing of pride and beauty,
but also the dignity of human consciousness aware of its ultimate end,
are described with unflinching realism. Even the composition is free
from concessions to grace or harmony: everything is jagged and torn.
Riccio's *Old woman seated* (iii) is often taken to be an ancestor of this
sculpture. Yet this earlier piece is by comparison merely picturesque.
Only Rodin expresses the human tragedy to its full extent.

120 *The gates of Hell* 1880 exhibited 1900 bronze 5·5 × 3·7 × 0·84 m.
Rodin Museum, Philadelphia Museum of Art
In his great book on French Gothic cathedrals, Rodin expressed regret
at the passing of a world in which sculpture had its proper home. In
The gates of Hell he built an architectural world where his sculptures
could find refuge from an environment in which they could exist only
as solitary fragments. Overcoming the Classic tradition of the abstract
ground, the ground here is a fluid matrix from which the various
figures emerge in birth and sink back in death. The torment, loneliness
and fragmentary nature of human existence are here made into a major
theme of monumental proportions. The futile turmoil of the Inferno,
as described by Dante, has been resurrected in bronze.

121 *The gates of Hell* 1880 (model) plaster 105 × 60 cm.

122 *The gates of Hell* 1880 (detail)
121–2 Paris, Musée Rodin

123 *Torso of Adèle* 1882 plaster 15 × 47 × 25 cm.
Paris, Musée Rodin
No other modern artist has been so successful in expressing inner states
of torment, yearning, or joy by means of unabashed gesture. Even if
fragmented further than its actual state, the remnants would still be
eloquent of the mood at which the artist aimed.

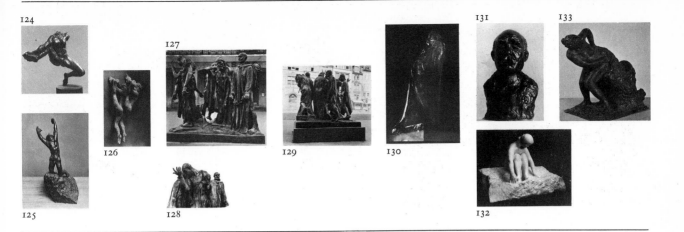

124

125

126

127

128

129

130

131

132

133

24 *Iris, messenger of the gods* 1890–1 bronze 34 × 26 × 30 cm.
New York, Joseph H. Hirshhorn Collection
By letting it reveal its organic principles of existence, Rodin discovered the unique integrity of the human figure. The living, spring-like motion of his *Iris*, animates and harmonizes its every member. Though this figure was conceived as centrifugally explosive, its unity is preserved by the proportion between mass and the force which emanates from the mass.

25 *The prodigal son c.* 1885 bronze with black patina 137 cm.
Oberlin College, Oberlin, Ohio, Allen Memorial Art Museum
R. J. Miller Jr. Fund
Normal orientation or even a horizontal relationship with the spectator no longer counts for Rodin. This figure, which is here fixed to a base at its knees, reappears in other contexts lying on its back or floating face down. There is no ideal point of view. Rodin's statues, being autonomous organisms, can be studied in all positions, from all sides.

26 *Le pas de deux c.* 1910–13 bronze 33 × 19 × 13 cm.
Paris, Musée Rodin
Like the capricious *Torso of Adèle*, these two figures, though obviously only fragments of a larger scheme, still form a complete world of their own. A spark of life-giving rhythm has been caught in these merging but nevertheless distinct shapes.

27 *The burghers of Calais* 1885–95
128 127 and 129 bronze 300 × 750 × 150 cm.
& Basle, Kunstmuseum
129 128 plaster 1884–6
Paris, Musée Rodin
'If I have managed to express the power with which the body longs to survive, and the force with which it has to battle with a generous soul, then I may congratulate myself on having done justice to the noble theme of the commission.' Not the heroic triumph of self-sacrifice but the struggle against the will to live became Rodin's theme as he worked on his most fully realized monument. It is for this purpose that he refused all traditional subterfuge: no dramatic composition – only the rhythm of figures isolated by anguish – and no heroic pedestal. The figures are 'to rub elbows' with the citizens of Calais. With incorruptible honesty, Rodin recognized the anonymity of modern sacrifice, and created a new martyrology.

130 *Monument to Balzac* 1897 bronze 275 × 92 cm.
New York, Museum of Modern Art. Presented in memory of Curt Valentin by his friends
Just as Balzac was obsessed with the most trifling details of his characters, so Rodin spent years in gaining as full a grasp as possible of the essentials of his subject. Rejecting the heroic nude, he achieved what amounts to a torso in reverse: only the head, neck, feet and hands, pressed through the dressing-gown, appear. The gown itself, though factual, is not treated as a relic. Instead it serves to metamorphose Balzac into a giant of legend whose outlines are too big to be grasped. Its rhythms and powerful slant give the whole figure a primordially sprouting effect, culminating in the immense head which regards the universe at an oblique angle, and from a distance, but with unequalled passion for all that is in the world.

131 *Clemenceau* 1911 bronze 46 × 28 × 28 cm.
Paris, Musée Rodin
Inspired by direct human contact with a reality which had to be dominated and conquered by his sculptural talents, Rodin produced some of his most masterly works. The daring clefts which separate the forceful thrust of bone and muscle through the skin do justice equally to the art of sculpture and the unique experience of a powerful personality.

132 *Beside the sea* 1910 marble 59 cm.
New York, Metropolitan Museum of Art, gift of Thomas F. Ryan
Unlike his fluent bronzes, Rodin's marbles, because they were cut entirely by his assistants, show a certain smug evenness of surface, a flaccidity of modelling, and a concession to the decorative, conventional tastes of his contemporaries.

EDGAR DEGAS
Paris 1834–1917
133 *Seated woman wiping her left side c.* 1900 bronze 35 cm.
'Madame Bovary, c'est moi.' Flaubert's exclamation was symbolic of nineteenth-century artistic attitudes which denied the integrity and

321

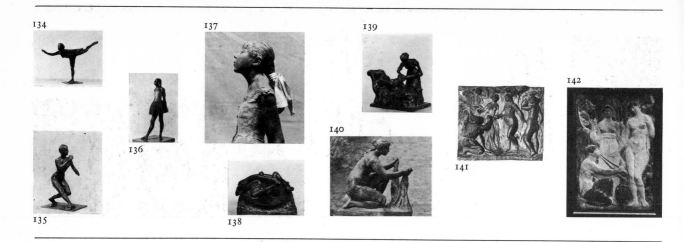

relevance of observed fact. Just as Madame Bovary is Flaubert, so the women modelled by Degas, though he had spent decades studying models, are all Degas. They have no life, no interest, no existence but that which he gives them. He even goes so far as to insist on showing us that the woman is no more important than the towel or the chair, and that each in turn is nothing but clay which has been differentiated just enough to let us recognize their shapes, but not enough to give them an autonomous existence.

134 *Arabesque over the right leg c.* 1890–5 bronze 20 cm.
Few artists of modern times have seized all the contradictory and limitless expressions of the human body with the precision of Degas. At once effortless and supremely controlled, graceful and contorted, indicating an expression of sheer will as well as giving direct proof of the instinctive beauty of natural motion, these studies of ballet-dancers have intrigued critics, connoisseurs and sculptors of the most varied and antagonistic schools.

135 *The bow c.* 1900 bronze 33 cm.
The spontaneous, liberating movement of the dance did not interest Degas. Instead he seized on the artificial gesture which is awkward seen from any angle but that of the orchestra seat. It is the intricacy of Degas's geometry which appeals at first. But, in counterpoint to the blank, indifferent female form which makes no appeal in its own right, even the geometry takes on tragic and sinister meanings. By reducing the importance of observed reality to nil, Degas opened the way to abstraction.

136 & 137 *The little ballet-dancer, 14 years old* 1880 bronze; skirt, muslin; hair-ribbon, satin 99 cm. (*see* IV, and note on p. 305)

138 *The tub c.* 1886 bronze 47 × 42 cm.
'When I tell myself that there once was a time in which painters painted Susannah in her Bath instead of Woman in a Bathtub . . .' Degas said. His rejection of the lovely, of the pleasing, was almost total and, in this piece, reached voluptuous aggressiveness. All angles and ungainly, cramped gestures, the nude is served up like a trussed animal on a common platter.

139 *The masseuse c.* 1896 bronze 42 × 38 × 30 cm.
The anonymity of his figures and the unprejudiced handling of composition allowed Degas an unparalleled freedom of construction. Having reduced his subject to a pretext which has no relevance outside the artist's perceptive imagination, he could deal with reality as he saw fit and without having to attain any pre-established degree of finish or resemblance to reality.

133–6 and 138–9 New York, Metropolitan Museum of Art. Bequest of Mrs H. O. Havemeyer, 1929. The H. O. Havemeyer Collection
137 Paris, Louvre

AUGUSTE RENOIR
b. Limoges 1841 – d. Cagnes 1919
140 *The washerwoman* 1917 bronze 120 cm.
New York, Museum of Modern Art
In his old age Renoir turned towards a monumental style and away from Impressionism. It was only natural that he should also turn to sculpture. Although these bronzes were not directly executed by Renoir, his genius speaks clearly from these full and tranquil forms.

141 *The judgement of Paris* 1914 bronze 74 × 87 × 17 cm.
Cleveland, Ohio, Cleveland Museum of Art. Purchase from J. H. Wade Fund
Striking a difficult balance between the earthy and the ideal, Renoir can induce even in a sceptical spectator an awareness of what is enduringly beautiful in the human form. The fragrant but never cloying warmth of his best canvases survives even in bronze.

CÉSAR CROS
b. Narbonne 1840 – d. Paris 1907
142 *Incantation* 1892 bas-relief coloured 34 × 24 cm.
Paris, Musée National d'Art Moderne
With its ideal of letting art penetrate into even the humblest objects of daily use, Art Nouveau asserted the possibilities of mass-produced art. According to this ideal, the artist, in the manner of a medieval craftsman, gladly gives up his individual prerogatives. Much admired by Rodin, Cros's architectural ceramic reliefs are among the best productions of this complex period.

145

147

149

150

146

148

PAUL GAUGUIN
b. Paris 1848 – d. Tahiti 1903

143 *Soyez amoureuses vous serez heureuses* 1889–90 painted wood 97 × 75 cm.
Boston, Mass., Museum of Fine Arts
Gauguin's flight to Tahiti stands as the most consequential example of Romantic rebellion against an intolerably materialistic world. It is also a symptom of a growing desire to return to the origins of culture. The whittled, dyed surfaces, the simplified forms as well as the sombre mood of these solemnly sensual figures lend this relief the vigour of fresh visions.

144 *Idole (à la coquille)* 1900 terre-vernisse 28 × 23 cm.
Paris, private collection
One of the most fundamental sculptures of modern times, this idol expresses a new desire for static, hieratic forms, later apparent in the work of Maillol and Brancusi. With its understanding of the inter-penetration of volumes, it points forward to Cubism and shows a decisive turning away from Realism.

GUSTAVE MOREAU
Paris 1826–98

145 *Lucretia* 1875–80 wax 20 cm.
Paris, Musée Gustave Moreau
One of the most enigmatic talents of the *fin de siècle*, Moreau is best known as a painter and as a great teacher. The supine and languid rhythms of Art Nouveau are latent here, but there is also a great sensitivity to free proportions and colour-evocative surface treatment, which lead on to the work of Matisse.

GIUSEPPE GRANDI
Val Gana 1843–97

146 *Monument to commemorate the Five-Day Insurrection of 1848*
Executed 1894 bronze
Milan, Piazzale delle Cinque Giornate
Contemporaneously with Rodin, Lombard sculptors were experiment-ing with 'open' forms of composition, powerfully animated, realistically observed figures, and a dramatic use of turbulently cleft surfaces. Though architecturally this monument is conventional, the powerful figures of

women, not insipid allegories, inciting the Milanese to rise during the tumults of 1848, have a fluency of motion worthy of greater attention than has been paid to the monument until now.

MEDARDO ROSSO
b. Turin 1850 – d. Milan 1928

147 *Sick boy* 1893 bronze 24 cm.
New York, Mr and Mrs Samuel Josefowitz Collection
Although likened to the Impressionists, it would be safer to associate Rosso with such artists as Monticelli and Moreau (145) because his lushness of textures and insistence on personal subject-matter prevents comparison with the true Impressionists. Nor is the strong reliance on light a matter of Impressionist technique, since Rosso used static arti-ficial light of calculated intensity when exhibiting his work.

148 *Conversation in a garden* 1893 bronze 33 × 68 × 40 cm.
Rome, Galleria Nazionale d'Arte Moderna
Rosso's work is still difficult to estimate properly. Freedom of composi-tion, first learned from his teacher, Grandi, and masterly technique in handling plaster and wax are Rosso's prime distinctions. The poetic interaction of delicately suggested atmosphere, though his most personal contribution to modern sculpture, is frequently haphazard.

149 *The bookmaker* 1894 wax over plaster 44 cm.
New York, Museum of Modern Art
Lillie P. Bliss Bequest
Rosso was able frequently to catch a wealth of fine nuances in his spontaneous interpretations of typically modern city characters. He was much admired by Rodin, but when compared to him or Degas, his art remains caught in provincial Italian traditions and his technique seems often motivated more by eccentricity than by deep and aesthetic convictions.

MAX KLINGER
b. Leipzig 1857 – d. Nuremberg 1920

150 *Beethoven* 1899–1902 marble, bronze and ivory 300 cm.
Leipzig, Museum der bildenden Künste
Art Nouveau, primarily a decorative movement, found its most concrete sculptural expression in Klinger's colourful, symbol-laden

memorial. The throne lends itself especially to the turbulence of expressive curves and disintegrating forms sinking into a restlessly heaving ground-plane. The figure itself is conventional and its hallucinatory quality is due to the fanciful setting.

ANTONIO GAUDÍ
b. Reus 1852 – d. Barcelona 1926

151 *Sculptural chimney-pots* 1905–7 cement, ceramic and glass ceramic
Barcelona, Casa Milá
The problem of integrating sculpture with architecture, after almost a century of disparate development, was partially resolved by Gaudí, whose plastic conception often allowed solutions which can be considered sculptural as well as architectural. In this respect, Art Nouveau was the first style of international importance after Neoclassicism, where a fusion of the arts was attempted.

152 *Figures from the portal of the Church of the Sagrada Familia* 1884 stone
Barcelona, Calle Provenza
Paradoxically, it was in Gaudí's figure sculptures that the attempt to bring sculpture and architecture together failed. His conventional treatment of the figures which fails to take up the dynamics of the wall against which they are placed shows he could achieve sculptural results only when operating as an architect.

ADOLF VON HILDEBRAND
b. Marburg-in-Hesse 1847 – d. Munich 1921

153 *Archery lesson* 1888 relief in stone 130 × 110 cm.
Cologne, Wallraf-Richartz Museum
One of the major theorists of the late nineteenth century, Hildebrand was the first sculptor to voice a reaction against wanton naturalism and the diffusion of detail. Insisting on compact forms seen from a single point of view, he achieved a new clarity of form deriving directly from Greek prototypes.

154 *The Wittelsbach fountain* 1844 stone
& Munich, Maximilian Platz
155 Although Hildebrand's treatise on sculpture points the way to abstract sculpture in its discussion of pure form, his works drained of literary

content, has an austere rhetoric which makes it the ancestor of all official sculpture. Aloof, humourless, relying on programme to offset spontaneity, his sculpture is the most inspiring example of modern bureaucratic art.

IVAN MESTROVIĆ
b. Vroolje (Yugoslavia) 1883 – d. America 1962

156 *Caryatids at the tomb of the Unknown Warrior* 1935–8 black granite
15·24 m. (whole tomb)
Yugoslavia, Mount Avala
The megalomania of the decades preceding the Second World War finds its expression in several historically, rather than aesthetically, important Government-sponsored monuments which blend a spurious peasant-like simplicity with aggressive nationalism. Programmatic, eclectic, meant to impress by its overwhelming bulk, this kind of sculpture met with tremendous success through the world, and set the style for Government-sponsored art.

PAUL BARTHOLOMÉ
b. Thiverval 1848 – d. Paris 1928

157 *Monument to the dead* 1899 limestone
Paris, Cimetière du Père Lachaise
This work, though it appears Academic to our eyes, had a profound influence in its day. Rebelling against Rodin's looseness of treatment, as well as against the detail-burdened Academic style, Bartholomé introduced a new Classic compactness and economy which paralleled the work of Hildebrand, and was decisive for the development of such later sculptors as Maillol.

158 *Tomb of Madame Bartholomé* 1887
Bouillant, Crépy-en-Valois
Anxious to raise sculpture to its former ethical and religious grandeur, Bartholomé experimented with a new intensive drama which eliminated the extraneous realism of contemporary sculptors. Taking up the ancient theme of love beyond the tomb, also the theme of Brancusi's *The kiss* (187), he combines it with the sanctifying presence of Christ on the Cross. But it is significant that the two groups do not merge in a drama of faith, love and resurrection. Christ, the mourning sculptor, and his dead wife all seem equally isolated from each other.

162

161

160

163

164

165

166

GIUSEPPE SACCONI
b. Montalto 1854 – d. Collegigliato 1905
159 *Monument to Victor Emmanuel II* 1885 (erected posthumously) marble, bronze and gilt bronze
Rome, Piazza Venezia
Its inner weakness disguised by unending bombast, this monument is perhaps the most perfect incarnation of late nineteenth-century rhetoric. Just as the architectural setting is illogical – the columns support no weight, the flights of steps lead nowhere – so the sculptural decorations are thrown together without any coherence or even legibility.

Adapted from a design for a lighthouse made by ANTONIO SANT'ELIA (1888–1916) in 1914; executed by Giuseppe and Attilio Terragni in 1933
160 *Monument to the fallen*
Como
Designed in the year that the monument to Victor Emmanuel was unveiled, but executed two decades later, impersonal, static, dissociated from everything organic, ambiguously suspended between 'pure' sculpture and 'pure' architecture, this work is prophetic of a mechanized future at the very height of *la belle époque*.

CARL MILLES
b. Lagga (Sweden) 1875 – d. Lidingö 1955
161 *Peace monument* 1936 Mexican onyx 10·97 m.
St Paul, Minn., City Hall
A spectacularly successful artist of our century, Milles presents us here with a precise record of fads in the official art world instead of arousing interest in his talent. Varying folk-lores, from Ancient Greek to Scandinavian to Mayan, indiscriminately retaining a certain sleekness of surface, he could reduce even Aztec gods to the strict conventions of chic.

GUSTAV VIGELAND
b. Mandal (Norway) 1869 – d. Oslo 1943
162 *Central obelisk c.* 1906 granite 16·76 m.
Oslo, Frognerpark
Perhaps the most enviable commission of this century, Frognerpark is a startling monument to perverse and unimaginative official taste. Super-

ficially streamlined to give them a spurious modernity, these figures might be considered amusing erotica if carved on a miniature scale. Bloated to monumental size and preaching Government-sponsored, cheerless *joie de vivre*, they appear false and arrogant.

PAUL MANSHIP
b. St Paul, Minn., U.S.A. 1885 – d. 1966
163 *Comrades-in-arms* 1953 bronze
Nettuno, American Cemetery
With its mawkish title, mindless realism and general aggressiveness, this monument recalls Italian Fascist sculpture of the 1930s, though it actually commemorates American soldiers who died combating Fascism. Bureaucracy and mechanization in contemporary life wreaks bitter ironies when called upon to create public works of art in celebration of death.

REG BUTLER
b. Buntingford, Herts. 1913
164 *Unknown political prisoner* 1951-2 bronze wire on plastic base 45 cm.
Berkhamsted, Herts., the artist's collection.
This is the most recent of those anonymous sculptures meant to commemorate the brutal mass destruction of man typical of our times, a series which begins with Thorvaldsen's *The Lion of Lucerne* (16). It is significant again that the total effect of this work was to depend more on its setting than on its intrinsic form.

ARISTIDE MAILLOL
Banyuls-sur-mer 1861–1944
165 *Mediterranean c.* 1901 bronze 104 cm.
New York, Museum of Modern Art
Maillol belongs to that generation which profited by but reacted against the example of Rodin. His earliest training in textile mills, and as a graphic artist, left him with a strong respect for severe, immediately comprehensible forms. Restrained, tranquil yet ripe with latent movement, his statues achieve an ideal impersonality.

166 *Desire c.* 1904 plaster bas-relief 117 × 113 cm.
New York, Museum of Modern Art
The sculptures of the pre-Classic Temple of Apollo at Olympia had a

325

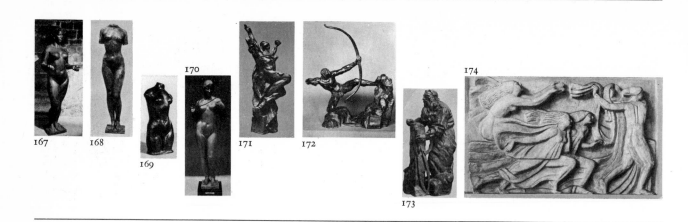

167   168   169   170   171   172   173   174

decisive influence on Maillol's style. The heavy massing of forms, especially in reliefs, reaching an almost geometric fullness, a certain brooding quality of oppressive maturity, and a rigid interlocking of forms straining against the frame are proof of the continuity in Maillol of the early Greek spirit.

167   *Pomona* 1910 bronze lifesize
Paris, private collection
This sculpture was originally intended for a funeral monument. Certainly the compassionate offering of the apples of immortality was used on countless antique *stelae* as a promise of afterlife. But more than the proffered symbols, the serene attitude of the figure itself has a quality of endurance, of familiarity with all that is abiding.

168   *Spring c.* 1910 plaster washed with blue 146 cm. (including base) × 41 × 25 cm.
New York, Metropolitan Museum of Art, Maynard Fund; from the Museum of Modern Art, gift of the sculptor
Though his style bears the imprint of his allegiance to Classical themes and forms, Maillol nevertheless remained French in his choice of proportions. Nowhere does this characteristic speak more clearly than in this slender torso.

169   *Small nude* 1910 bronze 20 cm.
Paris, Dina Vierny Collection
Maillol's vocabulary was limited and severe, yet he always surprises us with the flexibility and range of expression which can be derived from his basic theme, the female figure. In an age which clinically analyses the passions, Maillol was among the few artists whose faith in earth, flesh, and spirit remained unshaken.

170   *Woman with a necklace* 1918–28 bronze 174 cm.
London, Tate Gallery
Static massing of large volumes and smooth surfaces, so different from the style of Maillol's contemporary Bourdelle, is offset by a free and melodious silhouette. Commanding space by its powerful restraint, this Venus is among the most monumental works of the sculptor, capable of exerting its presence from some distance away.

ÉMILE-ANTOINE BOURDELLE
b. Montauban 1861 – d. Paris 1929
171   *St Sebastian* 1888 bronze 71 cm.
Paris, Musée Bourdelle
This very early sculpture reveals Bourdelle's admiration for, and spiritual dependence on, an expressive current of the French tradition which, sometimes mystic, occasionally lyrical and emotionally violent, persisted from the Gothic to the Renaissance and found its greatest Baroque exemplar in Puget (vii). Powerful surface modelling and pulsing forms impart a moody fascination.

172   *Hercules the archer* 1901 lifesize
Paris, Musée Bourdelle
The severe discipline derived from his experience of Ancient Greece, including Archaic, Classical and Hellenistic sculpture, enabled Bourdelle to control the more arbitrary impulses of his talent. Both in modelling and in composition a fine balance is struck between a maximum of mobility and structural clarity.

173   *Rodin at work* 1910 bronze 66 cm.
Paris, Musée Bourdelle
Charged with the crushing force of a boulder, this idealized portrait of Bourdelle's master also contains references to Michelangelo's *Moses* in the horn-like arrangement of the hair, the majestically impassive glance and the flowing beard. By means of this simultaneity of perception, Bourdelle transcends the portrait and achieves a monumental sculpture.

174   *Apollo and the Muses* 1912
Paris, relief on façade of the Théâtre des Champs-Élysées 284 × 440 cm.
Once having achieved an equilibrium between tradition and invention, Bourdelle was able to reconcile the conventional demands of public commissions with the demands of a very personal expression. In his reliefs he sought to '. . . integrate figure and wall so that the wall takes on human shape and motion and the figure gains the substantiality of the wall'. Clearly Hellenic in inspiration, the expressive freedom of distortion demonstrates a profound awareness of contemporary experiments in sculpture.

175   176   177   178   179   181   183

180   182   184

175   *Ingres* 1908 bronze 67 cm.
Paris, Musée Bourdelle
Bourdelle always admired Ingres who, like himself, was born at Montauban. Seizing at once on the impetuous, passionate nature of Ingres's personality as well as on the enormous discipline and intelligence with which this artist controlled the course of his own talent, Bourdelle has given us a masterly psychological study and a concrete expression of his own sculptural ideals.

176   *Hand of warrior* 1909 bronze 56 × 46 × 23 cm.
Paris, Musée Bourdelle
A student of Rodin, Bourdelle acquired from his master the gift of expressing the whole in a fragment. True Gallic eloquence of gesture depends on blending calculation with spontaneity. Here, though the subject is conventional, the strongly disparate proportions and the impressive silhouette are brought to harmonic resolution.

177   *Le fruit* 1911 bronze 226 × 110 × 70 cm.
Paris, Musée Bourdelle
A comparison with 184 reveals that Bourdelle was as drastic in his manipulation of proportion as was Matisse. The sinuous elongation of the torso, the wafting rhythm of outline and interior modelling gain their justification in the triumphant carriage of the head. The smile is expressed not only in the lips but in every part of the body.

178   *Little sculptress resting* 1905–6 32 × 26 × 18 cm.
Paris, Musée Bourdelle
Small in dimension but monumental in conception, this pensive muse embodies all the generosity of form, fluency of rhythm, and restrained surface ornamentation characteristic of Bourdelle's mature style. Especially in intimate works such as these, the vigour and serene liveliness of French Academicism continue to survive to our day.

CHARLES DESPIAU
b. Mont-de-Marsan 1874 – d. Paris 1946
179   *Paulette* 1910 bronze 41 × 30 × 20 cm.
Paris, Musée National d'Art Moderne
Despiau's work preserves an intelligent independence *vis-à-vis* the cross-currents of contemporary tendencies. Loosely allied to the serene

ripeness of Maillol, Despiau differentiated himself from this master by a greater accentuation of individuality and a lesser interest in generic concepts of structure.

180   *Eve* 1925 bronze 190 × 60 × 42 cm.
Paris, Musée National d'Art Moderne
Wistful nostalgia is offset by a robust love for attainable beauties, just as hyper-delicate surface modulations are balanced by a firm and very masculine judgement of the requirements of structure. Despiau is claimed by opposing factions in the art world but remains detached from aesthetic warfare.

HENRI MATISSE
b. Cateau-Cambrésis 1869 – d. Nice 1954
181   *The slave* 1900–3 bronze 95 cm.
New York, Museum of Modern Art, Mr and Mrs Sam Salz Fund
The influence of Rodin is clearly evident in this very early work. Yet in the restraint of gesture and in the far more stable volumetric conception, Matisse proved that he was already travelling a path characteristic of the early twentieth century.

182   *Copy of Barye's jaguar* 1899–1901 bronze 23 × 54 cm.
Switzerland, Theodore Ahrenberg Collection
Primarily a painter, Matisse was profoundly interested in sculpture from the very beginning of his career and prepared himself for both arts by freely copying the works of masters who held a special appeal for him. Barye's intense observation, lively surface modelling and massively fluent volumes are retained here but rendered with an even greater economy (*see* 73).

183   *Reclining nude III* 1929 bronze 20 cm.
Baltimore Museum of Art, Cone Collection
The ponderous motion of massive forms finds a peculiarly harmonic resolution in a work which, more than in any other of his sculptures, reveals Matisse's talent for a directness which combines apparent crudeness with refinement of thought and elegance.

184   *La Serpentine* 1909 bronze 57 cm.
New York, Museum of Modern Art, gift of Abby Aldrich Rockefeller

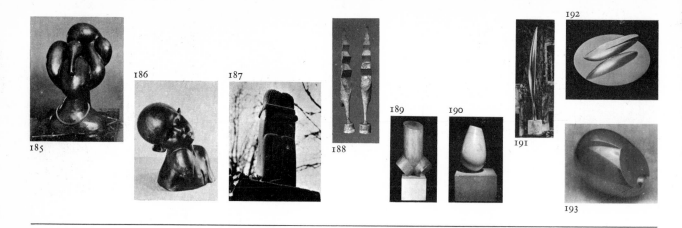

185

186

187

188

189

190

191

192

193

Matisse always discovered new proportions to convey purely sculptural rhythms. Although he liberated himself fully from the descriptive aspects of sculpture, he nevertheless achieved his fulfilment in a constant dialogue between natural appearance and the hidden, abstract principles of structure.

185 *Tiaré with necklace* 1930 bronze 20 cm.
Baltimore Museum of Art, Cone Collection
Following developments in his painting towards a more luxuriant style which lacked some of the primordial vigour of his earlier work, this sculpture has all the voluptuous ease of Matisse's maturity. Each form, in its swelling and subsiding motion, suggests all the attractions of the female body, and the conjunction of kindred forms is at once supple and disciplined.

CONSTANTIN BRANCUSI
b. Pestisuni Gorj (Rumania) 1876 – d. Paris 1957
186 *Head of boy* 1907 bronze 20 cm.
New York, Marlborough-Gerson Gallery
Dating from Brancusi's early years in Bucharest, this tormented study shows affinity with Dalou's *Head of sleeping baby* (107). But the faculty for intimate sympathy which later allowed Brancusi to discover the essence of animals and objects is already evident here in the treatment of every surface.

187 *The kiss* (tomb of Tanosa Gassevskaia) 1910 stone 125 cm.
Paris, Cimetière de Montparnasse
Brancusi's art, though it owes much to Rodin's emancipation of sculpture from the slavery of imitation, is one of severity and essential, concentrated form. The artist, instead of imposing his personality, has withdrawn in order to let his work speak for itself. This clinging, desperate embrace, which has been petrified by the passage of death, is the most poignant of all Brancusi's works. Man and wife have rarely been presented as being so completely of one flesh and one soul.

188 *The cock* 1941 bronze 103 × 21 × 11 cm.
Paris, Musée National d'Art Moderne
Not only the proudly raised pennant of the cock's comb but also his

shrilly ascending cry of triumph are irresistibly conveyed by the intricate interplay of serrated and smooth surfaces. The very stance of the rooster straining to launch his cry reveals the intimate understanding with which Brancusi projected the innermost characteristic of real or legendary animals.

189 *Torso of a young man* 1922 maplewood with limestone base 48 cm. plus 18 cm. base
Philadelphia Museum of Art, Louise and Walter Arensberg Collection
Compressing the physiological symbols of virility into the flexed torso of an adolescent and the rising growth of a tree, Brancusi has created a monument to the vital energies. The conflicting directions of the slanted ends add to the tense pride of all growing things, unveiling both the chastity and fertility of nature.

190 *Torso of a young girl* 1922 onyx with stone base 33 cm. plus 17 cm. base
Philadelphia Museum of Art, A. E. Gallatin Collection
The earth-bound, passive nature of woman in contrast to the tense activity of man is clearly expressed in this globular form which humorously suggests the awkward stance assumed by adolescent girls. But again it is the ferment beneath the surface, the pressure inside which urges on towards maturity and gives this sculpture its life and mysterious fascination.

191 *Bird in space* 1940 polished bronze 128 cm.
Venice, Peggy Guggenheim Collection
The swelling and diminishing profile suggests the rise and fall of a bird's song while the brilliantly polished surface catches and reflects changing streaks of light evocative of the swift, unpredictable course of birds skittering in a summer sky.

192 *The fish* 1924 polished brass height 30 cm. diameter 50 cm.
Boston, Mass., Museum of Fine Arts
Though retaining the general principles of the primordial fish in grey streaked stone (V), this fish moves with a quickly turning, quivering liveliness. The change of material, size, and pedestal are not simply playful variations but also logical necessities for the discovery of yet another aspect of the world of nature.

194 195 196

197

198

199

200 201

193 *The newborn* 1920 (original 1915) bronze 15 × 21 cm.
New York, Museum of Modern Art. Acquired through the Lillie P. Bliss Bequest
The quivering chin of the newly born crying as independent life is thrust upon it; the fecund ovum from which it begins the countless metamorphoses of gestation; the triumph of life which surges and subsides as prescribed in the cycle of birth, maturity, death and rebirth – these are only some of the themes summed up in the mystifying shape of the egg.

194 *King of Kings* 1937 wood 295 cm.
New York, Solomon R. Guggenheim Museum
Brancusi never scorned to profit by, and then transcend, the experience of other artists. Here the use of real objects, part of a winepress, suggests Cubist collage while the staring eyes and anthropomorphic aspect suggest Surrealism. But the commanding majesty of the figure, the implacable glance, reach into the realm of religious experience beyond aesthetic programmes.

HENRI GAUDIER-BRZESKA
b. Saint-Jean-de-Braye 1891 – killed on the Western Front 1915
195 *The imp* 1914 veneered alabaster 40 cm.
London, Tate Gallery
In his very short but astonishingly fertile career, Gaudier-Brzeska brought into focus many contemporary but differing sculptural experiments. In this example the artist has left Cubist influence behind, without surrendering the liberty to deal with forms arbitrarily, first revealed to him by Cubism. Many later developments are already foreshadowed here.

AMEDEO MODIGLIANI
b. Leghorn 1884 – d. Paris 1920
196 *Head of a young girl* 1913 bronze 25 × 20 cm.
Seattle Art Museum, Eugene Fuller Memorial Collection
At the beginning of his career, Modigliani was decidedly influenced by Cubism. Yet, even when he was most under this influence, his native sense of the indestructibility and dignity of all forms persisted. Harsh definition and simplification is apparent here, but the integrity and the humanity of the figure is preserved.

197 *Full length figure* 1908 limestone 160 cm.
New York, Gustave Schindler Collection
Modigliani, more than any other of his contemporaries, took the vogue for Primitivism with a grain of salt. Witty in its coupling of pure stoniness and provocative feminity, static as an idol yet definitely emerging from its husk, this is one of Modigliani's most accomplished works.

198 *Caryatid c.* 1914 limestone 90 cm.
& New York, Museum of Modern Art, Mrs Simon Guggenheim Fund
199 His restless life and undisciplined working methods prevented Modigliani from creating a sculptural *œuvre* which would demonstrate his great talent. He fully absorbed the Cubist experience of mass in motion being penetrated by space. Yet, while freely developing mass and voids in his sculptures, he never sacrificed his native realization that sculpture must strive towards monumental stability. Whereas the Cubist would shatter and then reorganize form in accordance with a new logic based on the ambiguous flow of time into space, Modigliani worked much more intuitively, modifying rather than destroying natural appearance. This caryatid strikes an astonishingly organic equilibrium between the free unfolding of sculptural volumes in space and the demands of a stringently limited, architecturally defined space.

200 *Head* 1914 limestone 46 × 27 cm.
New York, Perls Galleries
Certain of Modigliani's sculptures have the capacity to describe the states which occur in changes from animate to inanimate such as those which take place in the metamorphosis of insects. The expansion of the major spherical volume of the head bursting out of its shell of stone, itself hovering between organic and inorganic, like the half-sloughed skin of a snake, is here the dominant theme.

201 *Head* 1910–13 enville stone 62 cm.
London, Tate Gallery
Hieratic and absolutely still in its carriage, this head nevertheless has the incisiveness of a tomahawk swung through the air. By restricting himself to essentials and irreducible shapes, Modigliani here succeeds in suggesting, as Giacometti did later, external pressure acting on a solid and its resistance to this pressure, the solid thus retaining its form.

202

203

204

205

206

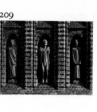

207

209

208

WILHELM LEHMBRUCK
b. Duisburg-Meideuch 1881 – d. Berlin 1919
202 *Standing youth* 1913 cast stone 230 cm.
New York, Museum of Modern Art, gift of Abby Aldrich Rockefeller
Lehmbruck is perhaps the only German artist of the first quarter of the
twentieth century whose medievalism is entirely personal. Ascetic
figures such as this one have an intensity of personal vision, an inner
logic of structure and a thoroughly resolved, highly expressive proportion which re-creates rather than emulates the meditative grace of
Late Gothic German carvings.

GEORGES MINNE
b. Ghent 1866 – d. Laethem-Saint-Martin 1941
203 *St John* 1895 bronze 71 cm.
Ghent, Musée des Beaux-Arts
Minne was perhaps the most important initiator of Expressionism in
sculpture, but his work is far too little known. His attenuated and
vulnerable figures surrounding the Folkwang Fountain in Essen were
of tremendous importance for Lehmbruck. In the present example,
Minne has proved his ability to preserve the powerful massiveness of
tone without sacrificing the brittle and spiky aspects which are so
characteristic of much of his work.

WILHELM LEHMBRUCK (*see* 202)
204 *Kneeling woman* 1911 cast stone 174 cm.
New York, Museum of Modern Art, Abby Aldrich Rockefeller Fund
A counterpoise to the angular, active figure of a man (202) whose rebel-
lious gestures are turned against himself. This figure of a woman is sub-
missive, graceful, in harmony with herself. Taken in conjunction, these
two figures make one think of the Annunciation theme, and it is
remarkable to what a degree Lehmbruck was able to infuse completely
opposed principles of expression within the same framework of formal
distortion.

205 *Female torso* 1918 bronze 78 cm.
Duisburg, Wilhelm Lehmbruck Museum
Much German art is concerned with finding an equilibrium between
the tormented, isolated self and the larger harmonies generally conceived of as Mediterranean. Here this Romantic element breaks through

to a rare resolution: Lehmbruck's strained and personal form is infused
with an idealized harmony. But the equilibrium was too difficult to
maintain. The artist committed suicide at the age of thirty-eight.

MOISSEJ KOGAN
b. Grgieiff 1879 – d. France 1942
206 *Female figure* 1933 bronze 37 cm.
Rotterdam, Museum Boymans-van Beuningen
An artist's artist, Kogan is now unknown to the public. But, among his
most exacting and famous peers of the 1920s and 1930s he was very
highly esteemed. Related to Modigliani and Lehmbruck, Kogan's art is
one of supreme sensibility. He spent years on the polish of a single
statuette till he had achieved the right relationship between surface and
volume.

ERNST BARLACH
b. Wedel-in-Holstein 1870 – d. Rostock 1938
207 *Cleopatra* 1904 ceramic 23 × 67 × 25 cm.
Hamburg, H. F. Reemtsma Collection
The sinuous form and exotic subject as well as the decorative character
of this early Barlach clearly belonged to Art Nouveau in which Barlach's
early experience is rooted. Stimulated towards greater expressiveness
and the more immediate and urgent appeal of German Expressionism,
and eager to exert a moral and religious function, he soon turned from
these beginnings.

208 *The ascetic* 1925 wood 70 × 32 × 32 cm.
Hamburg, H. F. Reemtsma Collection
Inspired by the heavily gouged woodcuts of the Brücke masters, by
folk art and whittled figures, Barlach's sculptures often look rough-
hewn as he exploits the humble nature of his material in order to
harmonize it with his themes of Christian abnegation and suffering.
The decorative elegance of his earliest style remains, though, diminishing the impact of his deliberate crudeness.

209 *Figures from the Church of St Catherine*, 1930–2 stone; left-hand figure
207 × 55 × 44 cm.
Lübeck
Surface modelling, which points up most clearly the dichotomy

210

212

211

213

214

215

216

217

218

---

between the sophisticated artist and the peasant carver he would like to be, is unimportant here because of the distance between the figures and the spectator. The spiritual affinity with medieval Germany is so great that there is little cleavage between the medieval building and its modern sculptural decoration.

KÄTHE KOLLWITZ
b. Koenigsburg 1867 – d. Moritzburg 1945

210 *Self-portrait* 1926–36 bronze lifesize
Berlin, Dr Hans Kollwitz Collection
Kollwitz is best known for her graphic work and her sympathy for the victims of all forms of totalitarianism. She followed the example of her acknowledged master, Daumier, in modelling a few small heads in which her strong emotional charge is recorded by means of a dramatic, but never selfconscious, struggle between dark voids and sharply defined volumes.

ERNST KIRCHNER
b. Aschaffenburg 1880 – d. Davos 1938

211 *The two friends* 1925–6 larchwood painted with tempera 175 cm.
Basle, Kunstmuseum
Eager to return to the virtues of medieval craftsmen, German Expressionists sought to re-create a folk art (*see* 207–9). But the febrile anxiety of the age, as well as the urban sophistication of the artist, were not to be suppressed. Real simplicity was never achieved by this group.

RAYMOND DUCHAMP-VILLON
b. Damville 1876 – d. in battle 1918

212 *Baudelaire* 1911 bronze 40 cm.
New York, Museum of Modern Art
Faceted with the precision of an impenetrable gem, this impassive and restrained portrait head is one of the noblest achievements of twentieth-century sculpture. An almost Egyptian aloofness and mystery reveal the fullness of Baudelaire's complicated genius.

SIR JACOB EPSTEIN
b. New York 1880 – d. London 1959

213 *Portrait of Dolores* 1923 bronze lifesize
London, Lady Epstein Collection

Virtuosity of surface treatment and precision in the definition of the individual forms give Epstein's portraits an uncanny liveliness. Though his style depends on an eclectic assimilation of the most varied traditions, his disdain for aesthetic programmes never allows aesthetic or critical concepts to dominate his fresh and highly differentiated images.

214 *Tomb of Oscar Wilde* 1912 Hoptonwood stone
Paris, Cimetière du Père Lachaise
In its exotic mixture of Assyrian, Greek-Archaic and Art Nouveau ingredients, this funerary monument is one of the few created in our century which clearly expresses the character of the deceased instead of simply repeating conventional funeral motifs. Though the Primitivism is deliberate rather than spontaneous, the totemic quality is genuine.

215 *Social consciousness* 1951–2 bronze 390 cm.
Philadelphia Museum of Art, Ellen P. Samuel Memorial, Fairmount Park Art Association
Bizarre archaisms and gestures which pass as mysterious when they are often merely puzzling are the hall-mark of Epstein's more monumental statuary. Composition, silhouette and grouping all have a singularly theatrical sense of posturing which contradicts the spontaneity of sentiment the artist strives for.

ARTURO MARTINI
b. Treviso 1884 – d. Milan 1947

216 *The prostitute* 1909–13 coloured terracotta 38 cm.
& Venice, Ca' Pesaro
217 Astonishingly ahead of its time, this sculpture incorporates the anxiety-ridden gesture, the surface and colouring of Expressionism with the formal discipline of the most advanced stages of Cubism (*see* nos. 219, 227). Each shifting viewpoint reveals an unexpected and autonomous harmony of expressive forms as well as an astonishing variety of inter-relationships between volume and void, between sharp, graphically traced outline and expanding or contracting volumes.

PABLO PICASSO
b. Malaga 1881

218 *The jester* 1905 bronze 41 cm.
Paris, Galerie Louise Leiris

219

220

221

222

223

224

225

In spirit and date this bust belongs to the Rose period. Picasso relies here on intuitive, passive sensitivity rather than on determined, active experiment. He is also exploring the world of his immediate predecessors, trying to assimilate their advances before plunging forward into the most phenomenal artistic adventure of our century, namely Cubism.

219 *Head of a woman* 1909–10 42 cm.
Paris, Galerie Berggruen
The disintegration of form observable in life, under the stress of motion and time, struggles here against the necessities of enduring sculptural construction. Whereas Rodin had decided in favour of the modification wrought by life, early Cubism strikes a balance between the two. A plurality of points of view, a depiction of volume as the hollow-contained as well as the shape-which-does-the-containing, the discontinuity of form, all these innovations are here fused with a finely calculated geometry of structure which gives each form its ideal, fixed shape – only to be contradicted again by changing the point of view.

UMBERTO BOCCIONI
b. Reggio 1882 – d. Verona 1916
220 *The mother* 1912 bronze 60 cm.
Birmingham, Mich., Mr and Mrs Harry Lewis Winston Collection
Boccioni is less cerebral and less controlled than Picasso (219) in his analysis of form, and in his exploitation of the interaction of disparate forms. Yet it was Boccioni who first formulated a programme of contemporary sculpture with which each new generation of sculptors has had to come to terms.

221 *Unique forms of continuity in space* 1913 bronze 110 × 86 cm.
Milan, Gianni Mattioli Collection
Muscles, and also the vectors of energy which they expend, are the protagonists here. The motion and direction of each form as it surges to its climax contributing to the pounding rhythm of the whole is here expressed anatomically but also with reference to the world of machines idolized by Futurists, as witnessed by streamlined form and insistence on machine-made polish.

222 *Development of a bottle in space* 1912 bronze 38 cm.
New York, Museum of Modern Art, Aristide Maillol Fund

Freed from Cubist discipline, Boccioni proceeds to give concrete form to the action of time and space on a familiar object. The bottle is clearly visible in the centre of the image but, at the same time, its disintegration under the impact of motion through space, and at a given tempo, are made equally manifest. The sculpture begins to devour the space which surrounds it.

ADOLFO WILDT
Milan 1868–1931
223 *The crusader* 1906 bronze 74 × 53 × 62 cm.
Milan, Francesco Wildt Collection
Futurism, to be fully understood, must be considered as a polemic campaign meant to revolutionize the masses. However, the sophistication of style and the heavy borrowing from Cubist theory made Futurist propaganda all but incomprehensible to the populace. The ferment which the Futurists desired to spread was manifested in more readily assimilable form by Wildt who combined the *avant-garde* with the reactionary. His torso, while being shown symbolically as a hollow cast, also refers back to the *Torso Belvedere*, much as the Futurists combined a progressive love for machines with the most retrograde chauvinism.

224 *Self-portrait* 1908 marble 38 × 32 × 20 cm.
Florence, Galleria degli Uffizi
Leaving behind all the brilliant intuitions and perceptions of Boccioni, those artists who were sponsored by Fascism retained all the bombast of Futurism without its vital mobility. As the most tormented official artist of the twentieth century, caught in the contradictions of a political scheme in which he had become enmeshed, Wildt had one of the most fascinating destinies of our times. Nowhere else can the drama of artist and officialdom be studied in all of its turgid refinements. Vigeland, Mestrović and Milles are his next of kin, but they belong to a mercantile rather than an artistic class.

GIACOMO BALLA
b. Turin 1871 – d. Rome 1958
225 *Boccioni's fist – lines of force* 1915 metal on wood base 80 × 85 cm.
Rome, Luce Balla Collection
Though primarily a painter, Balla experimented with sculpture. He

226

227

228

229

230

231

233

232

arrived at more audacious positions than Boccioni by completely avoiding visible reference to real objects. Instead, he used polished wire or sheet-metal to trace the trajectories of ricocheting movements and gives Futurism its purest sculptural expression.

RAYMOND DUCHAMP-VILLON (see 212)

226 *The horse* 1914 bronze 100 cm.
New York, Museum of Modern Art, Van Gogh Purchase Fund
Profiting by Cubist experience which allowed the artist to portray the interior as well as the exterior of a given volume, thus establishing a dynamic relationship between containing form and space contained, Duchamp-Villon here celebrates the irrepressible triumph of the machine. The beat of driving-shafts, the precarious balance of objects moving at high speed are conveyed with great strength.

JACQUES LIPCHITZ

b. Druskieniki (Lithuania) 1891
227 *Man with mandolin* 1917 stone 75 cm.
New Haven, Conn., Yale University Art Gallery, Société Anonyme Collection
Precise cutting of sharp edges gives these early sculptures the severe relations of key to lock, static and dynamic at the same time (*see* p. 43).

228 *Sailor with guitar* 1914 bronze 78 × 21 cm.
Philadelphia Museum of Art
Profiting from the dissociation of form created by early Cubism in its search for a mode of representation which would reveal a given object from a variety of positions, Lipchitz begins to integrate these experiences into a sculpturally stable form, while steering clear of experiments in transparent materials.

229 *Pierrot escaping* 1927 iron 49 cm.
Zürich, Kunsthaus
Having mastered a severe idiom for the exploration of space, time and volume, Lipchitz advanced to a new position in which he could express emotional or narrative content. The enigmatic, crystalline sculptures are superseded by more humorous, personal statements in which a hallucinatory element begins to appear.

HENRI LAURENS

Paris 1881–1951
230 *Man with a pipe* 1919 stone 37 × 24 cm.
Paris, Galerie Louise Leiris
As in Cubist painting, the strong intellectual discipline required of the artist produces a curious anonymity. However, where Lipchitz in his Cubist works tends to be passionately severe, and deliberately proposes for himself very difficult proportions, Laurens is more concerned with decorative analysis of form and a tasteful, often witty equilibrium of converging blocks.

231 *Red and black sheet iron* 1914 20 × 30 cm.
Paris, Mme Maurice Raynal Collection
Laurens is one of the discoverers of the flexible, characteristically modern material of sheet iron. By means of a trenchant analysis of the relationship between mobile masses and interpenetrating voids he achieves a curiously contradictory effect: starting with the most opaque and dull of metals, he finishes with a transparent and graceful sculpture.

232 *Tomb of the artist and his wife* (designed 1941) bronze
Paris, Cimetière de Montparnasse
In his later years Laurens succumbed more and more to facile rhythms and sluggish harmonies produced by bloated forms. Sometimes the very fullness of his volumes defeats his purpose. Instead of suggesting ripeness his forms merely appear as inflated balloons. A decidedly anthropomorphic bent and a slackness of imagination distinguish his later work very sharply from Arp, whose sculptures are all too often likened to those of Laurens.

ALEXANDER ARCHIPENKO

b. Kiev 1887 – d. New York 1964
233 *Standing figure* 1920 hydrostone 19 cm.
Darmstadt, Hessisches Landesmuseum
Whereas the preceding sculpture shows a certain interest in the Futurist themes of dynamic struggle, this figure, closer to Cubism, depends not on overt motion but on the dynamics of architectural parts and voids interacting and interpenetrating. The theme becomes a pretext for carefully calculated, completely satisfying resolutions of forms balanced exactly between motion and rest.

234

235

236

237

238

239

240

241

242

234 *The metal lady* 1923 brass and copper 75 × 50 cm.
New Haven, Conn., Yale University Art Gallery, Société Anonyme Collection
Elegance of profile and of material, as well as the strong internal rhythms, interpret the more strenuous speculations of Cubism in terms of easily recognizable human forms. Still, the pleasing syncopation and clever manipulation of highly economical shapes have a decided effectiveness. Slighter of inspiration than his revolutionary contemporaries, Archipenko can rise to an almost Classic balance between convention and innovation.

235 *Boxing match* 1935 terracotta 78 cm.
Venice, Peggy Guggenheim Collection
Moving away from Cubism's speculative investigations of form and space, Archipenko concentrated on laying bare the essentials of mass, void and movement. Here the angular thrusts, the curved masses of the predominating shapes suggest the punching arms and contracted back muscles of the adversaries who appear in the guise of the energies they expend, locked together by their mutual antagonism.

OSSIP ZADKINE
b. Smolensk 1890 – d. 1964
236 *Monument – the destroyed city of Rotterdam* 1953–4 bronze 6·4 m.
Rotterdam, Blaak, Schiedamse Dijk
An early explorer of Cubist techniques, Zadkine is primarily noted for his exposition of Cubist sculptural ideals in a decorative form which found wide public acceptance. In this late work a greater dramatic impact makes itself felt in the jagged, torn shapes, and the violent gesture of desperate defence and supplication.

237 *Mother and child c.* 1918 marble 60 cm.
New York, Joseph H. Hirshhorn Collection
The counteraction of sharply syncopated, interlocking motions seen as jagged forms and the serene blossoming of the rounded breast, which appears on the left and is repeated convexly on the right, give this work a piquancy unmarred by the superficial elegance which so often intrudes in Archipenko's more ambitious works.

ELIE NADELMAN
b. Warsaw 1882 – d. New York 1946
238 *Standing bull* 1915 bronze length 28 cm.
New York, Museum of Modern Art, gift of Mrs Elie Nadelman
Developing his inclination for acute observation and a sharply graphic interpretation, Nadelman renounced experiment in favour of a superficially elegant and blandly sophisticated style. Underneath this brilliantly decorative surface, however, a highly original and very daring sculptor is at work.

239 *Woman at the piano c.* 1917 wood stained and painted 89 cm.; base 57 × 24 cm.
New York, Museum of Modern Art, Philip L. Goodwin Collection
Without polemics, Nadelman introduced elements into American art which are still fruitfully at work. Fully grasping the American milieu and the American mentality, Nadelman created sculptures which are living samples of American life. At the same time his magnificent sense of proportion, gesture, and dynamic counterpoint of disparate forms adds the piquancy of a European tradition.

PABLO GARGALLO
b. Maella (Aragon) 1881 – d. Reus 1934
240 *Picador* 1928 wrought iron 24 cm.
New York, Museum of Modern Art, gift of A. Conger Goodyear
Fiercely Spanish in his insistence on the implacable density of his material, but quite without the speculative side of Picasso, Gargallo uses Cubist concepts in order to insist on the centrality of the human figure. Instead of drawing closer to abstraction by means of formal analysis, he imposes concrete realities on the Cubist idiom.

GEORGES BRAQUE
b. Argenteuil 1882 – d. Paris 1963
241 *Woman* 1920 plaster 20 cm.
Paris, Galerie Louise Leiris
In Braque's paintings the sculptural element is reduced to its most subtle minimum. This effect he translates into his sculptures which are almost all in relief. His intelligent yet spontaneous interplay between line, silhouette, and mass is of remarkable sensitivity and brings a touch of Classical harmony into a design which is full of modern syncopations.

243

244

245

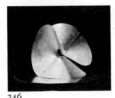

246

247

248

249

LASZLO MOHOLY-NAGY
b. Bacsbaisod (Hungary) 1895 – d. Chicago 1946

242 *Mobile sculpture* 1943 Plexiglass and chrome-plated steel rods 83 × 60 cm. Chicago, Ill., Mrs Morton Zurcher Collection
Moholy's work always maintains a certain affinity to the work of Gabo and the Constructivists. This resemblance also makes itself felt in his use of lucite and other synthetic materials which catch and mould light-beams into pure sculptural shapes. Compositionally Moholy distinguishes himself by a slightly more organic trend than the calculated perfections of Gabo.

NAUM GABO
b. Briansk 1890

243 *Head of a woman* 1916–17 celluloid and metal 61 × 48 cm. Middlebury, Conn., the artist's collection
Following Cubism, which conceives of volumes as contained space rather than as mass and which establishes line not as a silhouette but as a trajectory, the Constructivists created an analytic sculpture in which the hollow shapes formed by thin sheets of metal or celluloid represent the essential masses while the edges of these sheets trace the lines of energy which bind the various forms.

ANTOINE PEVSNER
b. Orel (Ukraine), 1884 – d. Paris 1962

244 *Torso* 1924–6 plaster and copper 75 cm. New York Museum of Modern Art, Katherine S. Dreier Bequest
Whereas Gabo tends towards a sublimated, musical harmony, Pevsner's sculptures even at his early analytical stage have something more anthropomorphic which is reminiscent of Duchamp's paintings. Not only are the structure and quintessence of a form given here, but there remains a mute, human expressiveness which makes itself felt especially in the forward bending of the figure.

NAUM GABO

245 *Monument for an institute of physics and mathematics* 1920 glass and bronze 60 cm.
U.S.S.R.
Gabo's sculptures are always midway between architecture and music. In this magnificently sober yet witty construction, which is just as much an assemblage of laboratory instruments as it is pure construction of arithmetically measured forms, he has also inserted a kinetic element of movable parts contrasting with the static structure.

246 *Translucent variations on a spheric theme* 1937 opaque plastic 56 cm. Middlebury, Conn., the artist's collection
Evanescent as a burst of the Northern Lights and expressive of a natural structural order inherent in all organic things, flowers, snowflakes, radiations, Gabo's mature style moves towards a Pythagorean sense of harmony in which beauty is serenely suspended between enduring stability and never-ending motion. He makes visible the incorporeal splendour of geometrical thought and intuition.

247 *Linear construction No. 2* 1942–3 plastic 60 cm. Middlebury, Conn., Miriam Gabo Collection
Just as the human eye gathers diffused light and channels it, so this dilating, contracting cat's-eye pupil, constructed of transparent materials, catches the light and makes it flow in clear rhythms. All the crystalline perfection of a mathematical structure is expressed, but also the exuberance of light which brings life to all it touches.

248 *Construction in space* 1955–7 steel covered with bronze. Middle sculpture in stainless steel, base covered with Swedish granite 25·35 m.
Rotterdam, N. V. Magazijn De Bijenkorf
Like a resilient, transparent seed-pod, this sculpture has at its centre a denser and more complicated organism alive with lateral and upward thrust: the sprouting germ, still cradled in its shell but about to grow beyond it. Convolutions of space, lines of growth, and solid volumes, keep their individual integrity, yet are resolved in a general harmony.

ANTOINE PEVSNER (see 244)

249 *World construction* 1947 brass and oxidized iron 75 × 60 × 57 cm.
Paris, Musée National d'Art Moderne
Pevsner's mature work, as rigorous as that of his brother, Naum Gabo, nevertheless retains a temperamental inclination towards the sensuous and visible, especially in his symbolism. Dense but luminous surfaces, activated by radiating striations of suffused energy, produce an effect of tension which is then resolved in the harmoniously grand silhouettes and in the tranquillity of the contained space-forms.

335

250

252

251

253

254

255

256

GEORGES VANTONGERLOO
b. Antwerp 1886 – d. France 1965

250 *Equation in chrome* 1935 38 × 15 cm.
Basle, Kunstmuseum, Emanuel Hoffmann-Stiftung
Vantongerloo attains the absolute stability and nicety of a complex algebraic equation. When a seed-crystal is dropped into a saturated solution, it creates a pole round which a large crystal can grow. Vantongerloo's sculpture acts somewhat in this manner: it polarizes unshaped and fluctuating space, centring it on the spare, crystalline shape of metal. Rigid and schematic in itself, his sculpture attains drama by its constant and forceful dialogue with surrounding space.

OSKAR SCHLEMMER
b. Stuttgart 1888 – d. Baden-Baden 1943

251 *Abstract figure* 1921 nickel-plated bronze 107 × 67 cm.
Stuttgart, Frau Tut Schlemmer Collection
Schlemmer was an outstanding teacher of mural painting at the Bauhaus. Although he accepted the importance of mechanization in our day and also believed in a craftsmanlike approach, his work was never reduced to schematic formulae. In all of his work one can feel the personal desire for order and a decisiveness in responding to one's surroundings.

GEORGES VANTONGERLOO (see 250)

252 *Construction in an inscribed and circumscribed square of a mile* 1924 cement 25 × 25 × 35 cm.
Venice, Peggy Guggenheim Collection
Independent shapes collide, interpenetrate and are mutually changed by their passage through one another. These collisions, however, are ideal rather than corporeal and produce no violence. The similar use of such logical stability of masses relying on each other has an especial importance for the asymmetric harmonies of De Stijl architecture.

JOSÉ DE RIVERA
b. 1904 West Baton Rouge, Louisiana

253 *Blue and black construction* 1951 aluminium 60 × 65 × 75 cm.
New York, Howard Lipman Collection
Revolving slowly on its motorized base, this work achieves a continuity of highly diversified forms which enclose and disclose ever-changing

varieties of space-shapes. This allows the silhouette to swell or diminish, relinquishing and embracing space. The strong but subtle colour contrasts between inside and outside surfaces help to articulate the complicated interplay of its changing positive and negative shapes.

RUDOLF BELLING
b. Berlin 1886

254 *Sculpture* 1923 bronze, partly silvered 48 cm.
New York, Museum of Modern Art
Using highly polished, machine-tooled elements of starkly geometric shape, Belling created sculptures that echo the robots of contemporary German Expressionist drama. This work evokes both fear of mechanization and involuntary admiration for sleek, clockwork beauty. It also produces a weird hallucinatory effect in the swivelling eyes which record everything and yet remain impassive.

MAX BILL
b. Winterthur (Switzerland) 1887

255 *Transition* 1958 chromoted brass 40 × 60 × 6 cm.
Zürich, the artist's collection
Blending mathematics and artistic intuition, Bill here represents a spiral plane twisting away from and back into a field of the same material. Although superficially a concrete representation of an equation, the immobilized yet charged spiral has a peculiarly maddening effect of suspense.

256 *Rhythm in space* 1962 (original 1947–8) granite 150 × 145 × 50 cm.
Dallas, Texas, Mr and Mrs Clark Collection
Bill's art is governed by the double purpose of exploiting modern themes of a mechanical-mathematical nature and that of rediscovering the nature of sculptural forms in motion through space. Spiralling round an unseen core, this piece displays a satisfying continuity of form which is always recognizably the same, yet always changed by the point of view.

PABLO PICASSO (see 218)

257 *Glass of absinth* 1919 painted bronze with silver spoon 21 cm.
New York, Museum of Modern Art, gift of Mrs Louise Smith
The 'real' object, placed in apposition to the 'created' one, heightens

257   258   259   260

261

263

262

the imaginative factor in the latter by means of sharp contrast. But at the same time, the real object, torn from its familiar context, takes on an existence of its own which is dependent on the new surroundings into which the artist has placed it. The process is analogous to that of collage, and also involves the blending of sculpture and painting. However, the assertion of the 'real' as an art object in itself has not yet been reached. Like some powerful and insidious octopus, a modelled object (the glass) reaches into the world of everyday reality, snatches a spoon, and absorbs it into its own organism. Dada and Duchamp in many ways reverse this process. A bottlerack (258), impelled by the will of the artist, propels itself out of the sphere which is its proper habitat, that of a practical utility, and plants itself in the world of speculative imagination.

MARCEL DUCHAMP
b. Blainville 1887
258 *Bottlerack* 1914 iron 58 × 37 cm.
Paris, Man Ray Collection
Mocking the sterile Academic reproduction of reality, but also the Cubist preoccupations with analysis and speculation, Duchamp boldly presents us with reality itself – but a reality altered by having been chosen by the artist and torn from its functional context (*see* above).

259 *Ready-made: Why not sneeze, Rrose Sélavy?* 1921 marble blocks, wood and cuttlefish-bone base in enamelled birdcage 11 × 22 × 16 cm.
Philadelphia Museum of Art, Louise and Walter Arensberg Collection
This object heralds Surrealism in its bringing together of disparate and antagonistic objects which are imprisoned in a cage, itself a prisoner of the artist's imagination. There is also the element of physical disorientation: when lifted, the lumps of sugar reveal themselves to be of marble, thus silencing those critics who insist that art should be imitation.

MERET OPPENHEIM
b. Basle 1913
260 *Fur-covered cup, plate and spoon* 1936 fur etc. cup 11 cm. diameter, plate 23 cm. diameter, spoon 20 cm. long
New York, Museum of Modern Art
This calmly disgusting object has become one of the classic objects of modern art and represents an important change from Duchamp's

cerebral, aesthetically selfconscious use of the ready-made. Whereas Duchamp's works are aloof and almost disembodied, a new branch of Dada turned towards new goals by furiously provoking the spectator's emotional, or at least visceral reaction.

KURT SCHWITTERS
b. Hanover 1887 – d. Ambleside (Westmorland) 1948
261 *Mermaid's purse* 1942–5 eggshell on a skate 16 × 23 cm.
London, Lord's Gallery
Just as sculpture often tends to become more pictorial in the twentieth century, so painting often becomes sculptural, until the limits between these two arts are eliminated by Duchamp's *The large glass* (VII). Collage becomes overtly sculptural with Schwitters, who insists that his art is not one of analysis, as is the art of Cubist collage (257), but a world of synthesis in which the jetsam of daily life is used – much as rubble from a burned house can be utilized for the foundations of a new construction.

LAURENCE VAIL
b. Paris 1891
262 *A quoi rêvent les jeunes filles* 1962 oil and lead wire on glass
Venice, Peggy Guggenheim Collection
Among the earliest practitioners of a technique which has proved immensely fruitful in recent decades, Vail derived his process from collage and from Surrealist constructions. There is in all of his assemblages a distinct comment on the modern scene in its commercial, psychological and social aspects. But it is the comment of a dream world.

LEE BONTECOU
b. Providence, R.I., 1931
263 *Untitled* 1961 welded steel and canvas 181 × 165 × 63 cm.
New York, Whitney Museum of American Art
The distinction between sculpture and painting tends to diminish in the last two generations of artists. These crater landscapes (or perhaps we are looking into mine-shafts – the direction of Bontecou's space is ambiguous), constructed as they are of wire raised from a canvas ground, participate in the art of painting yet surge upwards into sculptural space.

264

265

266

267

268

269

270

271

272

JOSEPH CORNELL
b. Nyack, N.Y., 1903

264 *Pharmacy* 1942–5 wooden case, glass bottles 35 × 30 cm.
Venice, Peggy Guggenheim Collection
Setting out from the experience of the Dada ready-made, Cornell has created a hermetic, intensely lyrical world in which poetic intuition gives order and harmony to lost and wandering fragments that come to the artist, no one knows whence. In Cornell's boxes, these lovely samples of reality find a haven and in turn emanate a sense of enduring peace and repose.

265 *Bleriot* 1954–5 construction 46 × 28 × 12 cm.
New York, Eleanor Ward Collection
The wound spring isolated against a neutral, impassive ground will never lose its pent-up energy just as the act of courage accomplished by Bleriot, the lone pilot will never lose its audacity – even if it should be forgotten. Gallantry and modesty are preserved for ever beyond the reach of chance.

LOUISE NEVELSON
b. Kiev 1900

266 *Nightscape* 1959 6 black units (wood) 118 × 240 × 20 cm.
Zürich, Gimpel and Hanover Gallery
Nevelson's assemblages of implements and woodwork decoration have a bewitching air of having been called together by a mysterious magnet which only attracts unexpectedly compatible elements out of an unending mass of Victorian debris.

JEAN ARP
b. Strasbourg 1887 – d. Basle 1966

267 *Periods and commas* 1943 painted wood relief 100 × 140 cm.
Basle, Kunstmuseum
Emanuel Hoffmann Stiftung
Arp arrived at his first mature sculptural style by the exercise of the Dada and Surrealist method of scattering unrelated forms within a field. These accidental arrangements, born by chance, were then transmuted by the artist into more disciplined compositions in which forms rise or sink between the pressure of larger colour areas.

268 *Siren* 1942 bronze 45 × 34 × 23 cm.
New York, Burden Collection
Though Arp allows a maximum of spontaneous development in his sculptures, the master's presence is nevertheless felt in the family resemblance which each of his sculptures bears to the next. More than any other modern sculptor, Arp fathers his sculptures and, like a wise father, he allows them to grow up individually.

269 *Silent* 1942 marble 34 × 14 × 11 cm.
Meudon (S.-et-O.), the artist's collection
Arp's genius consists in discovering new forms of organic life, each one of which functions with a biological logic that is always convincing and extraordinarily expressive of mood.

270 *Ptolemy* 1953 limestone 103 × 53 × 43 cm.
New York, Burden Collection
Though most of Arp's sculptures have an invincibly organic character, he sometimes allows a geometric precision to participate in the development of these living forms. Here, the geometric element is present more in the voids than in the volume.

271 *Garland of buds* 1936 pink limestone 48 × 38 × 28 cm.
Venice, Peggy Guggenheim Collection
Sometimes Arp allows the associational meanings of originally haphazard forms to rise to the surface. The swelling forms must have suggested the blossoming quality of breasts to him, and he developed this meaning until it is barely recognizable. The autonomous nature of the sculpture, independent from the object it describes, is maintained especially in the fluctuating space of the centre.

ISAMU NOGUCHI
b. Los Angeles 1904

272 *Kouros (in 9 parts)* 1944–5 pink Georgia marble – slate base 293 × 85 × 105 cm.
New York, Metropolitan Museum of Art, Fletcher Fund 1953
The smooth marble, in which each form defines one of the space dimensions and the erect stance, are in keeping with the title. But the freedom of intuition, the handling of space as an inalienable function of mass is in keeping with Brancusi, Noguchi's friend and master.

273 *Hiroshima Bridge* (new parapets on existing bridge) 1952
Island of Hiroshima, connecting it with the mainland
All the elegance of silhouette, all the lightness of touch and all the
sprightliness of Japanese architecture (which is always an eminently
sculptural architecture) are here united with the clarity of Western
engineering. In an age which tends towards fragmentation, the unity
between two major arts (where in this bridge does sculpture end and
architecture begin?) is a rare event.

JOHN B. FLANAGAN
b. Fargo, N. Dakota 1895 – d. New York 1942
274 *Early bird* 1941 bluestone 43 cm.
Estate of Curt Valentin
Together with Calder, Flanagan is among the first American sculptors
of international significance. His unfailing gift for letting the predeter-
mined shapes of field stones associate themselves freely with processes
of natural growth and metamorphosis give his sculptures a primordial
impact. The hewing seems to be done not by an artist's hand but by
time and erosion which leave only the core untouched.

FRITZ WOTRUBA
b. Vienna 1907
275 *Reclining figure* 1960 bronze 59 cm.
New York, Marlborough-Gerson Gallery
Wotruba's figures are small in actual dimension but their effect is always
monumental. This impression is due primarily to the highly original
infusion of architectural structure into human figuration. In this case,
the broken elements of the figure are comparable to the scattered
column drums of a ruined temple. Their coherence is implied, despite
their momentarily disjointed appearance.

HANS AESCHBACHER
b. Zürich 1906
276 *The harp* 1950 stone 210 cm.
Zürich, Hospital Gardens
This immense runic hieroglyph, dignified and yet playful, is hewn from
a field stone which seems to be rooted in the earth and suggests mythical
ages. It is an enigmatic musical instrument which can be played only by
the sun or the wind.

277 *Face abstraction* 1945 stone 32 cm.
Zürich, the artist's collection
As the embryo strains against the surrounding placenta, so the anonymous forms which can only be guessed at within the volume of stone
strain against the integument of the stone's surface. Relationship between surface and form is turned into a dark and disquieting struggle
symbolic of the bursting of the seed-shell, of the obscure transition from
inanimate to organic.

ALBERTO GIACOMETTI
b. Stampa (Switzerland) 1901 – d. Chur (Switzerland) 1965
278 *Project for a passage* 1932
Zürich, Giacometti Foundation
One's interest is immediately engaged by the fascinating equilibrium
between the visceral and the mechanical which gives this piece a puzzling quality. Giacometti often deliberately disorientates our sense of
scale. The complete lack of reference to outside reality forbids comparison with any other experience, and thus it is extremely difficult to gauge
the scale which might be monumental or diminutive.

279 *Invisible object* (vide, maintenant le vide) c. 1934–5 bronze 153 cm.
Saint-Paul-de-Vence, Maeght Foundation
One of Giacometti's earliest figural sculptures, this already shows a
decided whittling away of substance which characterizes the artist's
later style. A reminiscence of the mechanical aspects of his earlier work
lingers, especially in the hands which seem like electric terminals.

280 *Female figure* 1946–7 bronze 155 cm.
Venice, Peggy Guggenheim Collection
Elongated and compressed as if under the weight of the surrounding
atmosphere, this figure seems to be at bay, eroded to the core. One
expects her to vanish altogether, and yet she persists in existing. The
corroded surface is reminiscent of a dripping candle. And like candles
these figures seem to gain their *raison d'être* in the act of consuming
themselves.

281 *Woman with her throat cut* 1949 (original 1932) bronze 86 cm.
New York, Museum of Modern Art
Limp and disjointed yet jagged in outline, this sculpture seems to

282

284

285

286

287

289

290

283

288

incorporate in itself not only the victim but also the instrument of aggression and the fierce, clawing battle before death. Overtones of a crustacean carcass abandoned on a beach heighten its poetry.

282 *People in the piazza* 1948–9 bronze 17 × 60 × 41 cm.
Basle, Kunstmuseum, Emanuel Hoffmann Stiftung
Their paths seem to cross, yet these strange personages lost in a tremulous void will never meet. Though the composition looks random but the sense of alienation has rarely been expressed with such incisive precision.

283 *Portrait of Diego* 1954 bronze 65 cm.
Saint-Paul-de-Vence, Maeght Foundation
Only the hard irreducible core of individuality remains in Giacometti's portrait busts and this individuality is so exasperated as to exclude the possibility of mutual understanding. Withdrawn, aware of their own dissolution, these portraits are at once static in their lack of expression and aquiver with the nervousness of barely contained anxieties.

MAX ERNST
b. Bruehl (Germany) 1891
284 *Lunar asparagus* 1935 plastic 166 cm.
New York, Museum of Modern Art
Since Surrealism depends on the tormenting evocation of dreams, sculpture with its palpable reality is a generally intractable vehicle for the Surrealist. Ernst is one of the few who can give his sculptures the aura of something so hallucinatory that even the sense of touch does not waken us. These pallid sprouts could occur in anyone's dream.

285 *The king playing with the queen* 1959 (original 1944) bronze 96 cm.
New York, Museum of Modern Art, gift of Mr and Mrs John de Menil
By giving these chess-players the aspect of being themselves chesspieces, Ernst evokes in us the suspicion of being surrounded by objects which, far from being inanimate, are capable of direct action. An inscrutable, stealthy logic underlies his figures, and threatens us by its latent menace.

286 *Streets of Athens* 1960 bronze 74 cm.
Venice, Peggy Guggenheim Collection
In a humorous vein Ernst seizes on a direct and naïve impression of

mother and child rendered from the child's point of view. Yet, in the simplified flattening of forms, there lies also the impulse towards creating idols, whose shapes inspire in us an involuntary shudder of awe. Atavistic impulses dredged from the unconscious link the modern sophisticate with his prehistoric ancestors.

JACQUES LIPCHITZ (*see* 227)
287 *Figure* 1926–30 bronze 213 cm.
Hudson, N.Y., the artist's collection
Rigidly static as an Easter Island mask, yet endowed with a pulsating rhythm in the linkage of its lower parts, this work represents a summit in the history of contemporary sculpture. The obsessive image owes its emotional impact to its hypnotically staring eyes. Coupled with this element of mystery is the opposite of mystery: a hard-edged clarity of construction. The massive forms are somehow irreducible, and by being so they attain an insistent authority which dominates surrounding space. Though never a *bona-fide* Surrealist himself, Lipchitz's style changed under the impact of Surrealist experiments.

288 *Mother and child II* 1941–5 bronze
New York, Museum of Modern Art, Mrs Simon Guggenheim Fund
Always concerned with the monumental, Lipchitz insists on an almost architectural symmetry. But the forms themselves have all the swelling, breathing quality of ripe organic things, and the disparity between structural restraint and burgeoning life gives a powerfully convincing impetus to every gesture.

289 *Blossoming* 1941–2 bronze 54 cm.
New York, Museum of Modern Art
Lipchitz's flight to America coincided with the beginning of his most mature style. Dwelling now on the mysteries of regeneration, Lipchitz discovered a solemn but lyrical style in which the surface is allowed greater decorative character. Half human, half plant, the majestic unfolding of forms, resilient and proud of their growth is a new theme in the artist's work.

290 *Here are the fruits and the flowers* 1955–6 bronze 42 cm.
New York, Marlborough-Gerson Gallery
In his latest works, which Lipchitz defines as 'semi-automatic', the

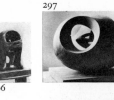

random forms shaped by the artist – and when the artist is a man of Lipchitz's experience no shape is ever really random – are allowed free development until they have grown to the point of demanding a more calculated intervention from outside. It is at this moment that Lipchitz, allowing poetic intuition to guide him, leads unconsciously germinating forms to their unforeseeable but natural fulfilment.

JOAN MIRÓ
b. Barcelona 1893
291 *Woman* 1950 bronze 32 cm.
Paris, Galerie Maeght
Miró uses surrealistic symbolism with great wit and frank sensuality. In sculpture he prefers the traditional clay shapes of Catalan crockery, freely associating the plump vessels proudly carried on the heads of peasant women with the women themselves.

HENRY MOORE
b. Castleford, Yorks., 1893
292 *Bird basket* 1939 lignum vitae and string 43 cm.
Private collection
Externally smooth and as unpretentiously attractive as peasant bowls, this arrangement of forms produces a variety of crossing axes and lends an asymmetric but harmonious twist to the space intervening between the volumes of forms. The intricate strings, besides defining axes and shaping the space, add the association of musical instruments.

293 *Head* 1937 Hoptonwood stone 52 cm.
New York, Martha Jackson Gallery
Landscape, enigmatic graphs, and physiognomy are only some of the keys which Moore gives us in order to solve this provocative riddle. Yet while we puzzle over this superficially attractive stone surface, we feel menaced by the disturbing watchfulness which emanates from behind the random peep-holes. The derivation from Mesopotamian sculpture only reinforces the arcane significance of this work.

294 *The warrior* 1953–4 bronze 150 cm.
Minneapolis, Minn., Minneapolis Institute of Arts, gift of John Cowles
Moore's disquieting, shrunken heads, just human enough to allow one to measure their degeneration under the pressure of fear, first appeared

in hundreds of drawings made in bomb-shelters. The fragmentation of the human figure reaches its ultimate expression in this mutilated creature which still maintains a last ditch defensive gesture before being utterly destroyed.

295 *King and queen* 1952–3 bronze 161 cm.
Antwerp, Middleheim Open Air Museum
Hieratically remote, and expressive of gallant expectation of catastrophe, these figures have become symbolic of the contemporary condition of mankind. Their vestigial heads are anonymous but their bearing still has a trace of regal dignity which justifies the title.

296 *Head and helmet* 1950 bronze 35 cm.
Venice, Ca' Pesaro
Experiencing the full impact of modern, mechanized war during the London Blitz, Moore began to work on sculptures which are powerfully enduring in the memory. This odd crustacean shrinking into his shell, terrified but also murderous, is among his finest works. Steelplate armour and the human form have inextricably intermingled.

BARBARA HEPWORTH
b. Wakefield, Yorks., 1903
297 *Large and small forms* 1945 Cornish elm 62 cm.
Private collection
The intimate seclusion of the mollusc in its shell, the logical development of swerving openings and silent caverns are typical of Hepworth's best works. Added to these qualities of organic inevitability of form is her rare gift for revealing all the beauty of colour, grain and surface of her chosen material.

KENNETH ARMITAGE
b. Leeds 1916
298 *The family going for a walk* 1951 bronze 74 cm.
Private collection
Somewhat dependent on Surrealist images, Armitage succeeds to an extraordinary degree in evoking not only the forms which are actually present but also the nature of their surroundings. The fragility of the figures huddled together is made poignant by the implied force of the sharp storm suggested by the inclination of the figures.

341

299

300

301

302

303

302

304

305

306

LYNN CHADWICK
b. London 1914

299 *Inner eye* 1962 wrought iron with molten glass 226 cm.
New York, Museum of Modern Art, A. Conger Goodyear Fund
The crystal held by rotating prongs suggests not only the eye of the title but also a central illuminating power which gives a germinal centre to the rest of the structure. With great originality, architectural elements and the sense of a sheltering cave have been associated with the anatomical reminiscences, the finely treated skin of the sculpture, and the grasping extremities.

ALEXANDER CALDER
b. Philadelphia 1898

300 *Mobile* 1934 glass, china and tea-cup handles 90 cm. diameter
Philadelphia, Pa., Philadelphia Museum of Art, Louise and Walter Arensberg Collection
Great charm is achieved here by suspending together a variety of objects of accidental treasure found on a beach, and by combining their exquisitely erratic motion within the limiting effect of the black frame which acts as a grand, stable foil. Sometimes these bits of brilliant glass and crockery clink together and produce a wistfully chiming sound.

301 *Josephine Baker* 1926 wire 100 cm.
New York, Perls Galleries
By using wire, Calder first began to open up his sculptures to their surrounding space, giving them a curiously vibrating life. In this example a syncopated rhythm, and nervy continuity of form, reproduce the scintillating movements of Josephine Baker and her snake-like gift of making a motion that begins at the hip and flows without change of tempo or intensity into her very finger-tips.

302 *Lobster trap and fish tail* 1939 steel wire and sheet aluminium 255 and 285 cm.
New York, Museum of Modern Art, gift of the Advisory Committee
Pursuing the logic of Futurism and Cubism which insisted on the necessity of integrating the modern dimensions of space and time into art, Calder was among the first to create sculptures which could be suspended rather than erected, and whose parts were so delicately joined that slight breezes were sufficient to animate them. Previous attempts at

setting sculpture in motion depended on clockwork (Baumeister) or on motors (Gabo) and gave a mechanical air to early mobiles.

303 *Whale* 1937 sheet steel 195 cm., base 163 × 120 cm.
New York, Museum of Modern Art, gift of the artist.
In his stabiles, Calder expresses contained rather than accomplished motion. A steady thrust seems to be the major theme in this case. The fragility of his mobiles appears here in a different guise: edges and planes are taut and only the spaces which form intervals between the iron plates have weight and massiveness.

GERMAINE RICHIER
b. Grans (Bouches-du-Rhône) 1904 – d. Montpellier 1959

304 *The bat-man* 1946 bronze 88 cm.
Hartford, Conn., Wadsworth Atheneum Collection
This hovering menace seems to decompose before our very eyes into its own veined and transparent phantom. The ambiguous sculptures of Richier, full of a dark humour, elicit as much terror as pity. When such creatures die, their power to terrorize does not end – it increases.

RICHARD LIPPOLD
b. Milwaukee, Wisc., 1915

305 *The spirit vine* 1957 copper wire enamelled in two shades of red, and platinum wire 220 × 165 cm.
Pauillac, Gironde, Château Mouton-Rothschild
Modulated, tremulous motion, rather than Calder's free sweeps are at the root of Lippold's finest work. Here the volatile bouquet, the scintillating colour surfaces, and the transformations which grape juice undergoes to become wine are all brilliantly brought to new life.

POL BURY
b. Haine-Saint-Pierre (Belgium) 1922

306 *Punctuation* 1963 wood and nylon 160 × 80 cm.
New York, Lefebre Gallery
Each white dot marks the end of a curved wire tendril which is made to move slowly over a short arc by a hidden mechanism. Lyricism and a certain innocence are arrived at here by means of motorization, marking a pleasant departure from the more baleful aspects of modern sculptors' encounters with machines.

307

308

309

310

311

312

313

314

315

VASSILAKIS TAKIS
b. Athens 1925

307 *Tele-sculpture* ball and electro-magnet 1959 39 × 37 × 31 cm.
Private collection
Like many contemporary sculptors, Takis takes up the challenge of machines. Instead of creating machines himself, as does Tinguely (349) or showing us their autopsy like Stankiewicz (343), Takis utilizes their energy in the form of the invisible but powerful magnetic field which holds various metallic objects in great tension.

JULIO GONZALEZ
b. Barcelona 1876 – d. Arcueil 1942

308 *Little classic head* 1910–14 bronze 27 × 20 × 15 cm.
Paris, Hans Hartung Collection
In his early work, Gonzalez revealed himself as a meditative, lyrical talent of great tenderness. Delicate surface treatment, ripe and sensuous forms and a slightly nostalgic Classicism give his work a contemplative *cachet*. Distinctly modern in his insistence on complete freedom in choice of forms, Gonzalez here has not yet developed into what he became in the early 1930s: a prime revolutionary of modern sculpture.

EDUARDO CHILLIDA
b. St Sebastian (Spain) 1924

309 *Enclume de rêve No. 10* 1962 iron sculpture on wood base 43 cm. (with base 149 cm.)
Basle, Kunstmuseum, Emanuel Hoffmann-Stiftung
Spain has always been the home of the finest work in forged or cast iron and it is no coincidence that in our century the Spanish sculptor Gonzalez, inspired by yet another Spaniard, Picasso, is responsible for bringing iron into the realm of modern sculpture. Today, this tradition is enriched by Chillida whose compositions are alive with an often aggressive drive to capture and clamp together a great variety of space-shapes.

JULIO GONZALEZ *(see 308)*

310 *Woman combing her hair* 1936 wrought iron 130 cm.
New York, Museum of Modern Art, Mrs Simon Guggenheim Fund
Encouraged by Picasso who had sought his technical advice, Gonzalez suddenly found his most personal expression in welded-iron sculpture. The intractable material must have delighted the Spaniard in him, as

did its lack of art historical tradition, i.e. its commitment to the twentieth century. The process of welding allowed all the freedom of modelling while retaining the monumentality of direct carving.

311 *Still life c.* 1927–9 iron 20 × 21 cm.
Paris, Mme Roberta Gonzalez Collection
All the sober dignity of traditional Spanish still life merges in this intriguing relief. Though the elegant sauce-boat actually exists in solid iron, its appearance is far more insubstantial and shadowy than is the bottle which is shaped out of air. A slight twist towards the spectator gives the whole sculpture an irresistible suggestion of pictorial space flowing in stately rhythms around all contours.

312 *Cactus-man No. 1* 1939–40 iron 69 cm.
Paris, Mme Roberta Gonzalez Collection
Just as the *Woman combing her hair* describes in a few arcs all the motions and gestures of complacent unity, so the *Cactus-man* fancifully reproduces the tough, enduring, virile element in nature. The negative spaces are static and columnar, and the tiny head and provocative manner of holding a cigarette suggest an 'apache'.

313 *Montserrat* 1937 sheet iron 162 cm.
Amsterdam, Stedelijk Museum
Gonzalez's supreme effort, one of the greatest achievements of modern sculpture, was inspired by the Spanish Civil War. The welded iron plates evoke the wrecked and antiquated military equipment of the Loyalists and the noble, courageous stance of the peasant defying danger in the skies is unrivalled as an expression of a nation's ideals.

ARTURO MARTINI *(see 216)*

314 *Woman at the window* 1941 terracotta 32 cm.
& Rome, Galleria Nazionale d'Arte Moderna
315 *The dream* 1931 terracotta 230 × 200 cm.
Acqui-Terme, Ottolenghi Collection
Condemned to work in an increasingly provincial, dictatorially brutal cultural environment by the Fascist government, Martini gave expression to the hopes and anguish of his times in a series of powerful yet infinitely fragile figures. In their immobility and breathlessness, these hushed groups preserve what is most valuable in the Italian spirit during a time of great crisis.

343

317

320

318

319

322

323

316

321

324

MARINO MARINI
b. Pistoia 1901

316 *Popolo* 1929 terracotta 115 × 80 cm.
Milan, the artist's collection
Marini is fully intent on resolving the dilemma of being true to Italy's ancient heritage, and to the demands made by the modern world which has severed itself morally and aesthetically from that very past. Here, in an early sculpture, Marini successfully translates a Roman theme, the ancestor bust, into modern form, giving his sculpture at the same time a deliberately political significance.

317 *Arcangelo* 1943 polychrome plaster 140 cm.
Basle, Kunstmuseum
This haggard figure, silently solicitous, is too substantial to be a spectre, and too remote to be quite human. Generally involved with a style of heavy, spherical volumes, Marini sometimes turns to a more direct and very eloquent realism which is saturated by a highly individual vision of human frailty.

318 *Igor Stravinsky* 1951 bronze 32 cm.
Minneapolis Institute of Arts
It is in his portraits that Marini reveals himself at the height of his power. The full mass of his shapes, the powerful, incisive manner of recording the passage of life over the most salient features of a face give each of his heads a convincing immediacy. The varied surface treatment, which sometimes threatens to become decorative in his more ambitious sculptures, is fully integrated in his portraits.

319 *Venus* 1938 bronze 110 cm.
Milan, private collection
Marini's devotion to the human form finds its most serene expression in a series of female torsos in which he recaptures his native Tuscan faith in the strengths and pleasures of the body.

320 *The miracle (horse and rider)* 1959–60 bronze 174 × 245 × 125 cm.
Zürich, Kunsthaus
The title probably hints at the conversion of St Paul. But the vision that this modern saint had had does not end in salvation, but in cringing despair. Even the surface, though it is not without its purely sensuous appeal, speaks of corrosion and dissolution.

GIACOMO MANZÙ
b. Bergamo 1908

321 *Grande cardinale* 1955 bronze 208 × 115 × 125 cm.
Venice, Ca' Pesaro
Manzù's sculpture is religious primarily because it is human. The shy withdrawal of the figure into the sheltering robes, the abnegation of attitude seems eloquent of faith in our time as a faith of 'despite'.

322 *Doors of St Peter's* commissioned 1952 cast 1963 bronze 7·4 × 3·6 cm.
Rome
Since the war many Italian cathedrals that had makeshift wooden doors have held competitions for modern sculptured bronze doors. Rarely has the break in tradition, the impossibility of inserting modern sentiments into the framework of a past monument been illustrated more dramatically. Manzù's solution is perhaps the most viable because of his very profound yet undemonstrative belief in the survival of Christian ethics.

BERNARD REDER
b. Rumania 1879 – d. U.S.A. 1963

323 *Lady with a house of cards* 1957 bronze 225 cm.
New York, Museum of Modern Art, gift of Mr and Mrs Albert A. List
Saturated with the mysticism and the robust sensuousness of his Talmudic heritage, Reder's images have a Baroque sense of unfolding. Each volume ripens in several dimensions at once, and each surface is alive with textural variations which depend on the tensions of underlying volumes. Intricate, highly poetic foreshortenings and cross-views increase the poetic liveliness of his works even further.

GIACOMO MANZÙ *(see 321)*

324 *Portrait of a lady* 1955 (original 1946) bronze 150 cm.
New York, Museum of Modern Art, A. Conger Goodyear Fund
Influenced by Medardo Rosso but more direct in his vision and far less dependent on ephemeral light effects, Manzù at his best can create an aura of intimacy which is all the more astonishing for its genuine monumentality. The smile on the face is drawn from a mood in which the entire figure participates.

KOREN DER HAROOTIAN
b. Armenia 1909

325 *Danaë and the shower of gold* 1960 bronze 65 × 117 cm.
New York, the artist's collection

325

331

333

327

328

329

330

332

326

Two contradictory factors, the inhuman brutality of Turkish oppression and that of Greek sculptural loveliness experienced as a child, when he fled from Armenia to Athens, have always dominated Der Harootian's work, which represents with great dignity the persistent tendency to honour the traditional sculptural idiom of human or animal forms, without ever losing sight of modern exigencies.

CONSTANT PERMEKE
b. Antwerp 1884 – d. Ostend 1956
326 *Marie-Lou* 1935–6 bronze 290 cm.
Antwerp, Middelheim Open Air Museum
Oppressively straining against the earth from which it has risen but of which it is still a part, this figure culminates in a fearfully mutilated face whose agony is a menace rather than a stimulant to compassion.

PABLO PICASSO (*see* 218)
327 *Skull* 1944 bronze 29 cm.
Vauvenargues, the artist's collection
Mortality, to most Spaniards, is the ultimate proof of life: only that which is capable of dying is capable of life. This skull, passive, inanimate, eternally dead, calls forth its opposite: life and the most important fact of life, its foreknown destruction.

328 *Shepherd holding a lamb* 1944 bronze 220 cm.
Philadelphia Museum of Art, R. Sturgis Ingersoll Collection
The patriarchal serenity with which Picasso has confronted the years after the turmoil of the Second World War reached its most profound expression in this bucolic group in which the harmony between man and his natural surrounding seems re-established. The forms are large and beautifully balanced without being forced and the pastoral tone is reminiscent of the Old Testament.

329 *Baboon and young* 1951 bronze 53 cm.
New York, Museum of Modern Art, Mrs Simon Guggenheim Fund
If death and destruction are important themes in the work of Picasso, life and creation are the necessary counterpart for a genius who is capable of grasping the extremes of existence. The mother's polished belly gives a singular splendour to the seat of regeneration, and the use of a toy car doubling as her snout adds a touch of simian exuberance.

330 *Owl* 1953 bronze 39 cm.
Estate of Curt Valentin
Few sculptors (Antoine Barye and Constantin Brancusi are among the exceptions) are able to deal with animals without falling into whimsicality. All the characteristics of a nocturnal bird of prey are captured in this sculpture. We are given the distinct personality of a shy, astonished, and wild thing that is fully aware of its power despite its humorous expression.

DAVID SMITH
b. Decatur, Ind., 1906 – d. Bolton-Landing, N.Y., 1965
331 *The letter* 1950 steel 95 × 58 × 23 cm.
Utica, N.Y., Munson Williams Proctor Institute
Profiting from the stubborn, muscular expressiveness of welded iron, and with these hieratic signals which boldly dominate space, Smith conveys a frightening urgency. His symbols are as baffling as the enigmatic writing of a highly sophisticated but vanished civilization.

MARY CALLERY
b. New York 1903
332 *Fables of La Fontaine* 1954
New York, Public School No. 34
Building on the new, free rhythms of welded and riveted metal, Callery's sculptures have a sprightly quality in which dance and gesture interweave. Here her figures appear in such a humorously fantastic aspect as to persuade us of their capacity to take any shape demanded by fable. All these qualities gain charm without losing their serious aesthetic intention in this commission for a children's play-yard.

ZOLTÁN KEMÉNY
b. Banica (Rumania) 1907 – d. Zürich 1965
333 *Spirit converter* 1963 brass 128 × 74 cm.
Zürich, the artist's collection
The relief ground breaks loose from its fixed position in the rear of the composition, taking on a shape preordained by the energy which has torn it loose, and drives forward and outward with exhilarating freedom. But for all the ambiguity of his fluctuating spaces, Kemény's control is always evident, especially in the harmony between motion and format.

345

334

335

336

337

338

339

340

341

DAVID SMITH (*see* 331)

334 *Head* 1938 cast iron and steel 50 cm.
New York, Museum of Modern Art
The linear relationships of these chunky elements tensely clamped together, suggest a powerfully impassive profile. At the same time, they seem to punch out corresponding blocks of space with great visual distinctness. Smith expresses all the intransigent toughness of the American experience in his cryptic sculptures.

MIRKO BASALDELLA

b. Udine (Italy) 1910

335 *Gates of the Fosse Ardeatine* 1950 bronze
Rome
Spiny, tormented, cruel, these gates open into a cavern outside Rome in which hundreds of hostages were shot. Their anonymity is preserved by the artist's refusal to personify their drama. Without shrinking from brutality, the artist presents us with the horror of modern extermination, perpetuating the moment of anguish rather than dealing in the facile coinage of patriotic condolence.

FRANÇOIS STÄHLY

b. Constance 1911

336 *Fountain* 1963 bronze 5·94 m.
St Gallen, Handelshochschule
Reversing the relationship of upward-jetting water and stable fountain support which is traditional in sharply vertical fountains, Stähly gives the two columns of polished bronze a tremendous rising impulse by means of the rhythmic projections. The water then glides downward, breaking into miniscule cascades against the serrated edges of the fountain.

CONSTANTINO NIVOLA

b. Orani (Sardinia) 1911

337 *Gods and humans* 1964 terracotta 40 × 40 cm.
New York, Byron Gallery
The massive fist of cloud and the fragile bodies just beginning to stir into life seem condensations of the vast, blank, unformed ground which has the imponderable capacity of dissolving into nothing or thickening into articulate, living form. The annihilating power of endless skies, of intense sun, the extremes of total aridity and smothering fertility, which

are part of Nivola's Sardinian heritage, are strikingly expressed in the wind-blown scope of his land-and-skyscape reliefs.

ALICIA PENALBA

b. Buenos Aires 1918

338 *Sculptures in concrete* 1963
St Gallen, Handelshochschule
This school of fish belongs to a remote race of mammoth life and seems to have been suddenly caught by fossilization gracefully drifting. An arcane past, a surprised present, and an enigmatic future are blended in a moment that is as witty as it is wise.

THEODORE ROSZAK

b. Poznan (Poland) 1907

339 *Chrysalis* 1936–7 metal and wood 50 cm.
New York, the artist's collection
Roszak's work matured during the 1930s and parallels Giacometti's Surrealist machines and models. Roszak invented a new and disquieting gender of forms which are a blend of the mechanical and organic. A curiously blind aggressiveness marks most of these works.

340 *Skylark* 1950–1 steel 248 cm.
New York, Pierre Matisse Gallery
This frightening pterodactyl has all the delicacy but also all the menace of fossilized bodies slowly coming back to life, though not to consciousness. Spontaneous invention is fused here with an almost biologically exact study of savage animals which once seen continue to haunt the memory.

JOHN CHAMBERLAIN

b. Rochester, N.Y., 1927

341 *Madame Moon* 1964 painted metal 48 × 74 × 53 cm.
Los Angeles, Robert A. Rowan Collection
In his disturbing assemblages which constantly change from recognizably familiar objects to abstract forms and back again, Chamberlain has found a strikingly bold representation of two conflicting yet concomitant phenomena typical of our civilization: mechanization and destruction.

346

342

344

345

347

349

343

346

348

JASPER JOHNS
b. 1930

342 *Light bulb* 1960 bronze 11 × 10 × 15 cm.
Los Angeles, Irving Blum Collection
The deadness of things, their mutability, and their eventual resurrection as pure form is celebrated by Johns. The familiar fragile light bulb becomes its own funeral effigy by being cast in bronze, but regains new life by turning from bulb into a satisfying form which evokes utterly new and sly associations.

RICHARD STANKIEWICZ
b. Philadelphia, Pa., 1922

343 *Untitled* 1961 168 × 90 × 85 cm.
Meriden, Conn., Mr and Mrs Burton Tremaine Collection
Inspired by Dada, and Surrealism, Stankiewicz creates emblems of our epoch of rapid consumption which turns even the most solid machines into junk. Stankiewicz associates himself with the traditional function of the artist as a transformer of reality. He composes with care and succeeds in inducing us to look beyond the actual material towards the unique image of his own conception.

ROBERT RAUSCHENBERG
b. Port Arthur, Texas 1925

344 *The bed* 1955 182 × 77 cm.
New York, Leo Castelli Gallery
Not since Crebillon's novel, *Le Sofa* has a piece of furniture revealed so much. But even after the brutal shock of the nakedly scabrous has passed, this bed retains its fascination and changes both its attractive and repellent aspects; sometimes it resolves itself into an abstract sum of colours, sometimes it appeals as a refuge from more conventional beds which seldom satisfy. Sometimes it speaks of a singularly American poetry of tawdriness.

GEORGE SEGAL
b. New York 1924

345 *Sleeping lovers* 1963 plaster and mixed media lifesize
Winnetka, Ill., Robert Mayer Collection
Like the casts of incinerated Pompeians made from the hollows produced in the lava of Vesuvius, Segal's sculptures imply annihilation of the objects they purport to represent. The people who modelled for these plaster casts are irrelevant. But their plaster replicas, incongruously and perpetually plunged into the barren continuum of their daily life, haunt us for ever.

ARISTIDE CROISY
b. Fagnon (France) 1840 – d. Paris 1899

346 *Le nid* 1882 marble lifesize
Paris, Musée de Montbrison
At its peak, nineteenth-century *Salon* realism in its relentless portrayal of detail and utter lack of personal comment strangely resembles some of the most advanced works (345) of today. But the divergences outweigh the similarities. The plaster cast paradoxically separates itself from reality while the scrupulous marble mimic of reality plunges us into totally diverse speculations and perceptions of reality.

FÉLIX DESRUELLES
b. Valenciennes 1865 – d. 1943

347 *Monument to four hostages* original 1924, destroyed 1941, reconstructed
& 1960
348 Lille, Boulevards Vauban et Liberté
Dada, Surrealism and Pop Art have opened our eyes to the meaningful effects of change. During the First World War five hostages were shot by the German army (only four seen on monument, one lay prone). In 1929 a mediocre monument was dedicated to the victims. In 1941 when the city was once again occupied a small mortar was set up in front of the monument and the hostages were executed a second time in effigy. Wisely this mutilated monument was preserved for it is perhaps the most eloquent memorial of modern war.

JEAN TINGUELY
b. Basle 1925

349 *Self-destroying machine* 1960
New York, Museum of Modern Art
The demonic aspects of mechanization spiced by a slight touch of scurrilous charlatanism appear in Tinguely's machines which do either nothing at all or else perform grotesqueries. In the self-destroying machine, which proved so delightfully inefficient as to require the artist's intervention during its *hara-kiri*, a climax is reached in the rivalry between sculpture and machine.

INDEX OF SCULPTORS AND WORKS ILLUSTRATED

Numbers refer to illustrations

349

FARNHAM SCHOOL OF ART